RENEWALS 458-4574

DATE DUE

Teaching
Our Children

WITHDRAWN
UTSA LIBRARIES

Nature gives to us her long-awaited production, placing him into the outstretched hands of the child makers. She gives her child to you, for you are THE CHILD MAKER. You are the representative of every human being, for all of us are makers. Each helps to mold, shape, strengthen, and weaken Nature's product, for whoever touches the child—be the touch warm and comforting or distant and restrained—affects the making.

Joel Macht

Teaching
Our Children
Joel Macht

University of Denver

JOHN WILEY & SONS, INC.
New York · London · Sydney · Toronto

LIBRARY
University of Texas
At San Antonio

Copyright © 1975, by John Wiley & Sons, Inc.

All rights reserved. Published simultaneously in Canada.

No part of this book may be reproduced by any means, nor transmitted, nor translated into a machine language without the written permission of the publisher.

Library of Congress Cataloging in Publication Data

Macht, Joel, 1938-
  Teaching our children.

  Bibliography: p.
  1. Behavior modification. 2. Children–Management.
3. Classroom management. 4. Parent and child.
I. Title.

BF637.B4M29   649'.1'019   74-13483
ISBN 0-471-56240-8
ISBN 0-471-56241-6 (pbk.)

Printed in the United States of America

10-9 8 7 6 5 4 3 2 1

To

Randy, Jobi, Kim, David
Carole
Eunice and Milton
Manny and Martha
Phyllis
Jimmy
Charles
and . . . Bea

Preface

This is a book for parents, parents to be, for children, and their teachers. Its sole purpose is to present ideas about how to teach children many types of behaviors. Its content will help you bring about some of the behaviors you believe appropriate for your children. Additionally, it will help your children to bring about some behaviors they desire from you.

It would be impossible to thank everyone connected with this book. So many people deserve more than my warmest recognition. I offer special appreciation to Drs. Lee Meyerson, Nancy Kerr, and Jack Michael, who helped me get my feet wet. I am grateful to Dr. R. Keith Van Wagenen for guiding me through a period that was not always pleasant for him. I thank Barbara Holzer and Don L. Wallin, who did much more than they will ever realize. And, the deepest of thanks to Kara, her parents, and again, Dr. Meyerson, all of whom gave me the opportunity to try to help.

Joel Macht

Contents

Teaching
Our Children

Introduction

Picture, for a brief moment, a friendly octopus. His arms are stretched in many directions. Each arm serves its purpose—providing substance for the body. So it is with psychology (not the most appetizing analogy, I suspect). We, too, have many arms or areas of interest. We investigate different ideas with the intent of providing the field of psychology with knowledge. Our arms, at times, disagree with one another. Some even try to deny the existence of others but, since we are attached to the same body, we all keep hanging around. Interestingly, we all, for the most part, have a common goal—that of helping.

This book will offer you ideas representative of one arm of our field. There are others, but I will confine myself to one because of my belief in it and my strong conviction of its effectiveness. I know that in a short while, you will see why I believe so strongly in it.

In the last 30 years or so, we have learned a great deal about human behavior. In my view, these last 30 years have been as productive as the preceding 100 years. One reason for the rapid growth of knowledge in the field of behavioral psychology is the way psychologists are now looking at human behavior. We have learned that under certain real-life situations, human behavior follows lawful patterns. This means that we are getting better at predicting when and why certain behaviors occur.

1

We are obtaining a clearer picture of some of the determinants of behavior. Finally, we are learning how to deal effectively with many of these determinants, and we are able to literally change behavior.

Psychologists are in the process of developing a technology of behavior. It is this technology on which the present book is based. This technology is emerging as a result, in part, of the work of such eminent researchers and scholars as Drs. B. F. Skinner, Donald Baer, Mont Wolf, Lee Meyerson, Gerald Patterson, Ogden Lindsley, and many others. Their work has enabled so many parents, teachers, and hospital personnel to make life better for an equal number of other parents, teachers, and children. This last statement is at the heart of the technology. Without question, one of the basic goals of behavioral psychology is to help people enjoy life more fully. For many, this goal has been accomplished. I do not wish to leave the impression that all behavioral problems have been solved. One quick look in any daily newspaper would certainly suggest otherwise. I do, however, wish to share with you my own optimism. Hopefully, by the conclusion of this book, you will share it with me.

You will realize one very curious thing about this technology as soon as you begin reading the main content. Much of what you and I will talk about is not at all new. You will recognize many of the suggestions, and you will undoubtedly say, "I've been doing that for a long time." Rest assured, your statement is correct. In fact, much of the information in this book has been known for thousands of years, and many parents, grandparents, and great-grandparents have been using it successfully for at least that long.

You may not agree with everything that is suggested, and that's fine. Most of us have very strong opinions and feelings about teaching and bringing up children, so disagreement is not only expected, but healthy. It is from disagreement that many new things are learned. Quite honestly, however, I will try to sway some of your opinions. I will attempt to convince you to try some ideas that you have perhaps never tried before. I will omit, whenever possible, such words as "right" and "wrong." Instead, I will tell you what will happen to a particular behavior when you do A or B or C. This will put you in a better position to decide what you believe is best for you and your child.

Ultimately, the purposes to which you will use the information provided in this book is in your hands. This technology that we will talk about is powerful. That is not meant to be an overly dramatic statement, but a realistic one. Personally, I have never set out to help parents change their children's behavior without first looking and discussing the potential long-range effects the program will have on the entire family. Please consider this last statement when you begin to develop a program for you and your children. Sometimes hastily thought out programs yield fruit that is not sweet. I will help you to avoid the lemon tree but, to do so, I will need your assistance and patience.

I have written this book with the hope of answering one question. Are there things you can do to make it easier to be a parent and more fun to be a child?

It's What Comes After That Counts

Thank goodness for Momma! Those were my exact words. I was sitting in the kitchen with my 22-month-old daughter. I had just made her an egg, which she refused to eat. She wanted a cookie. My seven-month-old son had just awakened from a nap and was softly crying in his room. I left the kitchen to get my son—which did not please my daughter. She still wanted her cookie. "I'll be right back," I said to her, wondering out loud if she understood what I had just said. I brought David into the kitchen and placed him in his chair. He was still crying. One of my senses told me he needed changing. "What should I do first," was the thought that came to mind. Where is the rightful king of the family? She was taking a shower. A door closed, and the sound brought a sigh of relief from me and the word "Momma" from my daughter. Thank goodness for Momma! It took about five seconds (seemed like five hours) for Momma to appear. During that brief period, my daughter once again reminded me of her desire for a cookie. I had forgotten. "Okay, stop your crying, I'll give you a cookie." It's amazing how a cookie in the mouth puts a "stop" to crying. Now that Momma was in the kitchen, peace and quiet returned. Quite suddenly, I began to laugh. My wife asked me what was so funny. "Do you realize what I've just done? Here I am writing a book on how to bring up children and I have just done something my readers have been advised against doing. I just gave Kim a cookie so she would stop her crying and all I did was to *tell* her to cry the next time she wants another one."

What I have just described— and it happened— is an honest admission that even those of us who think we are authorities still make mistakes. We accidentally teach our children to behave in ways other than what we really want. But let's face it, when you are by yourself with two crying children, knowing what to do and doing it can be worlds apart.

Most parents have experienced the same thing. Fortunately, these mistakes are made only occasionally, but we still teach what is desired. As we will see, we must try to keep our slips to a minimum. Otherwise we make our jobs as parents doubly difficult. In the above example, the chance was increased that my daughter would cry the next time I failed to give her what she requested. I didn't mean for this to happen, but my intentions did not matter too much. What was important was the way I responded to Kim's behavior.

Our child's behavior is greatly influenced by the way we react to what he has done. Our reactions help to determine whether our child will repeat his behavior or whether he will do something different. This statement is a very important part of a principle of behavioral psychology. The principle states that a behavior is influenced or affected by how the environment—people, places, and things— immediately responds to the behavior. Perhaps without realizing it, you have used this principle many times. On the occasion when you told your child what a good boy he was after he cleaned up his room, you used the principle. When you sent your child to his room for fighting with his brother, you used the principle. When I gave Kim a cookie after she started to cry, I used the principle. In each of these examples, a particular behavior occurred first—cleaning up a room, fighting, and crying. In addition, there was a reaction to each behavior—the child was praised, sent to his room, or given a cookie. By these actions, we have influenced the previous behaviors and have helped to determine whether those behaviors will occur again in the future.

Cooperation Between Mike and Patty

It seemed that Mike and Patty's playtime always ended up with Patty crying. It wasn't that they fought with one another, but whenever Mike started playing with a toy, his younger sister would grab for it. A tug-of-war usually developed with Mike being the winner. It was at that point that Patty would begin to cry. Mother's reaction was to take the toy from Mike, explaining to her son that since he was older, he should let his sister have the toy. There was little cooperative play between the two children, and Mother felt that something had to be done before Mike's feelings toward his sister became worse. A decision was made by the parents to try to teach their children to play with one another and to decrease some of Patty's crying.

For the next two weeks, Mother made a special effort to watch the children very carefully when they were playing. At the first sign of any sharing of toys or mutual play with a toy, Mother would immediately go over to the children, give them both warm hugs while telling them how good they were being for playing together. Occasionally, she would give each of them a cookie while they were playing together, again telling her children how happy she was to see them having such a good time.

When a situation arose where Patty attempted to grab one of the toys Mike was playing with, Mother would immediately walk over to her daughter and calmly tell her that she would not be able to play with any toys if she continued to grab what Mike was playing with. Sometimes this statement was enough, and the children again began to play together. When this was observed, Mother would immediately praise both children. When Patty began to cry, she was quietly taken to her room—where there were very few toys—and had to remain there until her crying stopped for about two minutes. When the crying did stop, Mother returned Patty to the toys in the family room. At the first opportunity, Mother praised both children for playing together.

As soon as Patty realized that her crying would no longer bring her a toy, the crying almost completely stopped. She and her brother learned that it was much more fun to play together than to fight over a toy. Cooperative play occurred more often each day. The children learned that their mother would respond to them in a very pleasant way when they played together nicely.

Although Mother was not aware of it, she was using the principle all along. Unfortunately, she was not using it to the benefit of herself or her children. Initially, she reacted to Patty's crying by giving her the toy. Mother was unintentionally increasing her daughter's crying by reacting to it as she did. When Mother changed the way she responded to her daughter's behavior, her daughter's behavior changed. Now cooperative play brought Patty what she wanted—the toys and a lot of praise and affection.

It appeared that the entire family benefited from the change. Certainly, Mother's job was made easier ("easier to be a parent . . ."). There was much less fussing between the children, and Mother had much more time to do what she needed to do. Additionally, the children were taught how to have more fun with each other (". . . and more fun to be a child."). Interestingly, the children began to do many more things together—to the delight of their parents. For this family, the goal of this book was accomplished.

Change does not always occur as rapidly as it did with Mike and Patty. Quite honestly, sometimes change does not occur at all. Without the patience and cooperation of their parents, Mike and Patty would probably still be having their tugs-of-war. The parents, in one sentence, had to look at what they were doing. Dr. Donald Baer, in a foreword for a very fine textbook[1] for teachers, has written:

> "To paraphrase a hero of our folk mythology, Pogo, 'We have met the causes of our behavior, and they is us.' We can (change) those causes and thereby change some behaviors." (Parentheses are mine.)

[1] Beth Sulzer and G. R. Mayer, *Behavior Modification for School Personnel*, Hinsdale, Ill.: The Dryden Press, 1972, p. vi.

Getting
Prepared

Parents as teachers of a child's behavior is far from a new concept. The teaching role begins from the moment Nature gives us our children. All of us have taught and are presently teaching our children to do or not to do many things. What the very young child learns is almost exclusively what his parents teach him. As he grows older, others begin to take part in the teaching task. Sometimes what our child learns is exactly what we have intended to teach him. Other times, we are not so fortunate. Accidental or unintentional teaching is quite common and, in many cases, the sources of the accidental teaching are not the parents. But accidental teaching can be undone, as well as being avoided. Let's see how.

How well do you know your child? Silly question? I'm not certain. I think you might be quite surprised. Try this suggestion. Take a few hours over the next two or three days and just sit back and watch what your child is doing. You don't have to look for anything specific—just be an interested observer. Watch him during the early morning hours, midday, early afternoon, late afternoon, dinner time, and finally at bedtime. Develop the habit—if you don't already have it—of looking at what your child does. It is critical that you catch your child doing something good. In order to do this consistently and effectively you are going to have to know what he does—both good and not so good.

Once you have completed this little task, I would like you to repeat it, only this time with a slight addition. Take a piece of paper and a pencil and divide the paper in half with a penciled line down the center. On one half write the word "good" or "desirable." On the other half write "not so good" or "undesirable." As you begin to watch what your little one is doing, write down a description of what you see in the appropriate column. If the same behavior occurs more than once put a mark by the earlier description. In this way, you will have a good idea of how often a particular behavior occurs.

These observations are very important. Every parent I work with is asked to do what you are now doing. It is interesting that many parents, having looked carefully at their children's behaviors, begin to see things that they haven't seen before. The number of *good* things sometimes comes as a pleasant shock. Additionally, many parents have remarked to me that the child who "misbehaves all the time" really doesn't! Believe it or not, that observation quickly brings about positive changes in the parents' attitude and behavior.

It will be helpful for you to read this book while you are thinking about one or two of your child's behaviors. You will be able to work mentally through some of the procedures before you actually try them—it's a good technique. Go through your lists of behaviors and pick a couple of them. Make certain that the behaviors you select are *observable*—those you can actually see happen. Let me give you a little help with this request. Assume that you have listed the following:

Good	Not So Good
1. Going to bed on time.	1. Not getting dressed on time.
2. Picking up toys.	2. Crying when told no.
3. Playing nicely with brother.	3. Disrespectful to sister.
4. Helping wash dishes.	4. Not showing responsibility.
	5. Playing with matches.
	6. Immature.

Just for practice, put a check mark by the above-mentioned behaviors that you can actually see happen. Did you select numbers 3, 4, and 6 on the not-so-good list? Most people would, but they are not really observable behaviors. They actually stand for observable behaviors. Ask yourself, what does my child *do* that tells me he is disrespectful, or immature, or not showing responsibility? When you have decided what it is that he has *done*, then you are probably talking about observable behaviors. Let me get picky. Look at number 3 on my good list. The word "nicely" doesn't really tell us a great deal. What does the child *do* that is nice? For me, he shares his toys; he doesn't grab one from someone else; and he does not push in order to get a toy. Those are observable behaviors—we can watch the child doing them. (You might not agree with my definition of the term "nicely" as used in number 3. That's fine, but what is yours?) One more quiz. Which of the following are observable behaviors?

1. Acting like a baby.
2. Thinking clearly
3. Doing homework.
4. Being stubborn.

If you only checked number 3, you earn an "A." If you guessed number 1, 2, or 4, ask yourself, "What does my child do that enables me to know he is acting like a baby, thinking clearly, or being stubborn?" When you answer the question, look at what you have said.

Look back at the behaviors you have selected to think about through the remainder of the book. Are they observable? In addition to checking them, ask yourself these questions. Does the behavior have to be changed? Would you and your child benefit from the change? You are the only one who can set the ultimate standards for your family's behavior, so think carefully about these questions. You must decide what is desirable and undesirable behavior for your children. If your decision creates problems, think about compromise. For a program to yield beneficial results for the entire family, the family must work together. If you are having difficulty thinking in terms of which behaviors, if any, need changing, discuss your situation with your family physician. He might be of some help. At the same time, think about this statement[2] from John and Helen Krumboltz's book "Changing Children's Behavior."

"For advice on what constitutes desirable behavior you may select from such sources as the Bible, the Koran, the Congressional Record, lists of educational goals, newspaper columns by Dear Abby or Ann Landers, Amy Vanderbilt's writings on etiquette, the behavior you learned from your parents and teachers, or the opinion of your next door neighbor. You are certain to obtain contradictory advice when you consult many different authorities, but we feel that constructing your own standards of desirable

[2] J. D. Krumboltz and H. B. Krumboltz, *Changing Children's Behavior*, Englewood Cliffs, N.J.: Prentice Hall, 1972, pp. xviii-xix.

behavior is very important . . . You must be your own judge of what behavior you think best prepares your children for the years ahead."

I am in complete agreement with them.

Increasing Behavior Using Positive Reinforcement

Why is it when we are not dieting, and we are hungry and know it is time to eat, we walk—or run—to the dinner table? Pretty foolish question, isn't it? Why do you think many of us put our glasses on when we decide to read a book or watch television? How about this one. Why do we insert our car key into the ignition switch of our automobile when we have to pick up the kids or go to the supermarket? The answers, of course, are obvious. In the first case, we obtain food; second, we can begin to see something; and in the last case, if we fail to put our key in the ignition we are going to have a hard time getting our car to go any place. Walking to the dinner table, wearing glasses, and using our key usually brings us results we desire. These desirable results or reactions guarantee that we will continue to do the same things the next time we want to use the car, see something, or eat at home.

In most cases, we no longer think about how we are being responded to by our environment; we take environmental reactions for granted. We are quite certain that a paycheck for our labors will come at the end of a week or month. We are equally certain that when we jump into a pool on a hot summer day, we are going to be cooled off. We predict (without thinking much about it) that by sitting next to a blazing fire, we will warm up.

But what happens to our behavior if the environment fails to react to us in a way that we perceive as desirable? Our behavior begins to occur less often, or it may not occur at all. If food was never again given to us at the dinner table, we would be less inclined to go to the table when hungry. If our paycheck was no longer forthcoming, most of us would have to stop working at that job and find another that would once again pay us for our work.

Many of our children's behaviors also occur because their environment provides desirable outcomes for their behaviors. If an 18-month-old child finds that he is given a cookie after saying "cookie" to Mom or Dad, the child will probably continue to say the word cookie. The same child may find that by saying the word book, he will, in many instances, be given a book. When an environment provides "thank you's" and appreciation for doing chores around the house, chances are doing chores will continue.

What would happen to a child's behavior if his environment no longer provided any positive outcomes for his behavior? The result would be the same as with your behavior or mine. The child's behavior would be less likely to occur.

We know that many parents strongly believe that children should do things for reasons other than positive outcomes. Perhaps they should—perhaps everyone should behave desirably for reasons other than reinforcement, even you and I. But that is a philosophical or moral issue that only you can decide. Consider your own behavior and the behavior of all the people you know. Can you think of someone who continues to put forth effort when a desirable outcome is never forthcoming? Although the reinforcers differ for many of us, the reinforcers are still there. Praise, affection, recognition, warm feelings, money, vacations, medals, good grades, most valuable player awards, power, and a host of other things are strong incentives for all of us. We work for these things. I wonder how logical it is to assume that our children should do otherwise.

SOCIAL REINFORCEMENT

Many parents believe that reinforcement is synonymous with candy, toys, or a new bike. They sometimes overlook the fact that the most important and necessary form of reinforcement is their own demonstrated attention, recognition, and affection. Without a parent's smiling, praise, and touching, family life would not only be sad, but unbearable, and we would have an almost impossible task of teaching desired behaviors.

Almost every child is willing to work hard to obtain attention. Attention and affection, then, are powerful aids for teaching. Although we all prefer to use our attention to teach what we think is best for our children, it doesn't always work out that way. Let's look at a couple of examples of how our attention is sometimes used and then look at how it should be used.

Billy and Miss McCawley

Miss McCawley was having difficulty with a seven-year-old in her second-grade class. She described the child as being very hyperactive. When asked what she meant by that term, she indicated that the child rarely remained in his seat. For over half of the one-hour period, he would walk around the room, occasionally stopping to talk with one of the other pupils. When the child's behavior was observed, two things were noticed. First, the other children refused to talk with Billy when he came over to them. Miss McCawley had told the other children to pay no attention to Billy, and they followed her instructions completely. Miss McCawley had informed the other children that she would be the one to discipline Billy. Second, when Billy was out of his chair, his teacher would remind him that he should be sitting. She would remind him about four times each hour. Additionally, when Billy returned to his seat, the teacher would nod her head in his direction and then continue on with her discussion or presentation. Within a short period of time, Billy would once again leave his chair.

It was suggested to the teacher that she might, accidentally, be maintaining Billy's wandering around the room. It was pointed out that possibly her verbal attention (telling Billy to sit down), which was given *when* the child was out of his chair, might be a stronger reinforcer than the nod given when Billy was in his chair. She agreed with this possibility.

Miss McCawley no longer reminded Billy to sit down. Instead, when he was in his chair she would occasionally walk over to him and while touching his shoulder, tell him what a good boy he was being for sitting so nicely. She would withhold her social reinforcement when he was doing what she didn't want him to do and give him a lot of attention and affection for behaving as she desired. By the end of the week, Billy was sitting in his chair for about the same amount of time as the other children in the class.

Teacher attention was a strong reinforcer for Billy. We know this because he was working hard—getting out of his chair—in order to receive it. Teacher attention was the environment's reaction to his behavior. Billy received the most attention *when* he was out of his chair. When the teacher began her new program—attending to Billy when he was seated—he sat in his chair more often. Take a look at the following chart. It presents a "before" and "after" picture of Billy's behavior, of Miss McCawley's reactions, and the resulting effects the teacher had on Billy's behavior.

Behavior	Environment's Reaction	Results
Behavior 1 (out of chair)	Teacher's reaction *A* ("sit down"— social reinforcer)	*Increase* in out-of-chair behavior
Behavior 2 (sitting in chair)	Teacher's reaction *B* (nod—little, if any, reinforcement)	*Decrease* in sitting-in-chair behavior
New Program		
Behavior 2 (sitting in chair)	Teacher's reaction *C* (praise, attention, touching)	*Increase* in sitting-in-chair behavior
Behavior 1 (out of chair)	Teacher's reaction *D* (no social reinforcement at all)	*Decrease* in out-of-chair behavior

Mrs. J. and Lisa

Mrs. J. was becoming annoyed at her three-year-old daughter's fussing and crying. This behavior occurred more and more each day. As a result, Lisa was spending quite a bit of time in her room as a form of punishment. According to Mother, sending Lisa to her room did not help very much other than to give Mrs. J. a little peace and quiet. In addition, Mother did not like sending Lisa to her room as often as she was doing. After talking with Mother for several hours and observing the way she was reacting to her daughter's behavior, the following was noticed.

A.   Lisa played by herself. She had no brothers or sisters. While she played, Mother would be busy cleaning up the house, preparing something for dinner, or sitting alone in the kitchen enjoying a cup of coffee. Occasionally, Mother would stop what she was doing to see if Lisa was all right. When Mother saw that her daughter was still playing, she would return to what she was doing usually with no comment to her daughter.

B.   When Lisa would begin to cry or whine, Mother would walk over to her and ask what was wrong. Lisa would usually ask for a glass of milk or a cookie. On several occasions, the child would not eat or drink what was given to her. This was apparently upsetting to Mother, for she would tell her daughter that she wasn't going to get anything else if she continued to be wasteful.

C.   If Lisa continued to cry, Mother would calmly take her daughter and place her in her room. She would tell her daugther that if she was going to cry for no reason she would have to cry in her room.

D.   After three or four minutes, Mother would bring Lisa out from her room. In almost every instance, Lisa would still be crying when she was taken out of her room. Mother would then do one of two things. She either gave Lisa a glass of milk or a cookie, or she would tell her daughter that she would have to go back to her room if she didn't stop her crying. The crying usually stopped, at least for the time being.

Mother was asked to evaluate the goal she had established for her daughter's playing. She was asked if she believed it was reasonable for a three-year-old to play by herself for two or three hours at a time. Mother agreed that this was probably asking too much. It was pointed out that Lisa was getting very little, if any, social reinforcement from her mother when she played by herself. On the other hand, Mother was talking to her daughter and offering cookies and milk when she cried. It was also pointed out that Lisa was taken from her room while she was still crying. Being removed from the room might be serving as a form of reinforcement, possibly maintaining some of the crying.

It was suggested that when Mother observed her daughter playing by herself, she should make a pleasant fuss about the behavior. Occasionally, she should go to her daughter and join her in some games. She should tell her daughter how good she was being for playing so nicely. She should offer Lisa milk and cookies when she was playing, not when she was crying. Finally, if Mother decided to send her daughter to her room for crying, Lisa should have to remain in her room until she stopped her crying for a few moments. Then she should be taken out, and Mother should socially reinforce the noncrying, quiet behavior. Crying decreased rapidly. Quiet behavior and game playing between Mother and Lisa increased rapidly. Equally as important, Mother did not have to send Lisa to her room as much as before.

Behavior	Environment's Reaction	Results
Behavior 1 (quietly playing by herself)	Mother's reaction *A* (no reinforcement at all)	*Decrease* in playing by herself
Behavior 2 (crying in family room)	Mother's reaction *B* ("what is wrong"— attention and social reinforcement, milk and cookies)	*Increase* in crying in family room
Behavior 3 (crying in bedroom)	Mother's reaction *C* (child removed from room while still crying—type of reinforcement)	*Increase* in crying in bedroom
Behavior 4 (crying after being removed from bedroom)	Mother's reaction *D* (milk and cookies, verbal warning— possible social reinforcement)	*Increase* in crying after being removed from bedroom
NEW PROGRAM		
Behavior 1 (quietly playing by herself)	Mother's reaction *E* (pleasant fuss— social reinforcement, attention and verbal reinforcement, join in game playing, milk and cookies)	*Increase* in quietly playing by herself; *increase* in Mother and Lisa playing together
Behavior 2 (crying in family room) or milk	Mother's reaction *F* (no social reinforcement, no cookies or milk)	*Decrease* in crying in family room
Behavior 3 (crying in bedroom)	Mother's reaction *G* (child remains in bedroom until she is quiet for a few moments)	*Decrease* in crying in bedroom

Behavior 5 (additional behavior— return to noncrying, playing quietly)	Mother's reaction H (pleasant fuss— social reinforcement, attention and verbal reinforcement, join in game playing, milk and cookies)	*Increase* in quietly playing by herself; *increase* in Mother and Lisa playing together

Although other types of reinforcement were used in addition to social reinforcement, Mother's attention, praise, and affection were very important aspects of Lisa's program. Mother began to understand how reinforcement can be used to increase many behaviors after she saw how she was responding to Lisa's crying. As with Miss McCawley, all Mother had to do was to change *when* she reinforced her daughter. Reinforcement was now given after Lisa did what Mother felt was best instead of when her daughter was crying. Additionally, Mother reevaluated her goals, and it appeared that Lisa was very pleased about that.

I now would like to present you with a third situation. This time, however, I am going to ask you to develop the program. The behaviors in question are running and walking in the house. I have supplied one possible answer, but understand that other solutions might be just as appropriate. (If you'd like, fill in the "blank" chart.)

Mike, I Believe I've Told You Once Before

Mike is five years old. You and I know his parents very well, and tonight we are going to have dinner at their house. Mike sits with us at the dinner table, and we are extremely impressed with his very pleasant and bright manner. After dinner, you quietly tell his mother what a nice young man Mike is. Mother responds, "Yes, most of the time." Within a few moments, all of us are sitting in the living room talking. Mike is asked to go watch television or play with his new building set. He reluctantly leaves the room.

All of a sudden, Mike comes running by us. As he looks our way, he begins to run upstairs—jumping two stairs at a time. Mother looks in the direction of her son. "Mike, I believe I've told you once before to stop running in the house." He quickly stops running and proceeds to walk the rest of the stairs leading to the second floor. Mother immediately turns to us and informs us that she has already told him five times today not to run in the house. After about three minutes, Mike comes charging down the stairs, streaking by us with a smile. "Michael," exclaims his mother, "what did I just tell you?" Mike apologizes and walks to his room, "Can I go back upstairs and watch television?" Mike asks from his bedroom. "Of course, you can," Mother says. Mike walks by us and goes up the stairs. Mother tells us that the running in the house is about to drive her up the wall. Everybody politely chuckles—except Mom and Dad. As if shot from a cannon, an object flies by us, and we can tell it was Mike by the color of the passing shirt. "Mike, you are embarrassing me in front of our friends. How many times must you be told not to run in the house? I will not tell you again." Once again, Mike apologizes and returns to his room.

What Mike's Mother Is Now Doing

Behavior	Environment's Reaction	Results
Behavior 1 (running)	Mother's reaction A	
Behavior 2 (walking)	Mother's reaction B	

Your New Program

Behavior	Environment's Reaction	Results
Behavior 2 (walking)	Mother's reaction C	
Behavior 1 (running)	Mother's reaction D	
Any additional behavior?	What should be Mother's reaction?	

When a parent is having some difficulty with her child's behavior, I immediately try to determine which of the child's behaviors is most often being responded to with social reinforcement. In many cases, the behavior causing the problem is the one generally gaining the most attention from the parents. In Mike's situation, his parents have been responding almost exclusively to his running, while not paying a great deal of attention to his walking. Unknowingly, and certainly accidentally, they are maintaining some of their son's running. My chart, therefore, would look as follows.

Behavior	Environment's Reaction	Results
Behavior 1 (running in the house)	Mother's reaction A ("stop running in the house"—attention, social reinforcement)	*Increase* in running in the house
Behavior 2 (walking in the house)	Mother's reaction B (no social reinforcement at all)	*Decrease* in walking in the house
	New Program	
Behavior 2 (walking in the house)	Mother's reaction C (a good deal of social reinforcement—attention, recognition, praise)	*Increase* in walking in the house
Behavior 1 (running in the house)	Mother's reaction D (no social reinforcement; perhaps a loss of reinforcement for a brief period of time— no television for five minutes)	*Decrease* in running in the house

Whether your program or mine were precisely the same is not too important. As long as you were able to see that Mike's running was receiving the most attention and his walking went relatively unnoticed, and you altered those relationships, then you have the point very well. I did not add an additional behavior, but you might have. If your addition was a desirable behavior in your eyes, did you follow that behavior with social reinforcement? I did, however, add another way for Mike's environment to respond—loss of TV time—which may not be necessary. Television did appear to be a strong reinforcer for him, and it's loss, as a result of running, might bring about a quick decrease in the running. The loss of television would *not*, however, solve the problem. Sooner or later, Mom is going to have to change *when* she is responding to Mike. Later, we will look at other factors that should be considered before one should remove reinforcement as a form of punishment.

We know that praise, attention, affection, and recognition are potentially powerful reinforcers. They can be used to help us increase the future occurrences of many types of behaviors. Unfortunately, many of us have fallen into the habit of using our attention and recognition for behaviors that we would just as well decrease. In a very true sense, we have developed the habit of ignoring the good child—more appropriately, his good behavior. With this last point in mind, look at the behavior you selected from your own list. If the behavior was taken from your not-so-good column, ask yourself if it is at all possible that your are responding to it as Miss McCawley, Mrs. J., or Mike's mother did with their target behaviors.

USING SOCIAL REINFORCEMENT EFFECTIVELY

Social reinforcement will be extremely effective if you will keep three ideas in mind. First is the idea of immediacy. The closer the reinforcer is to the behavior, the greater the chances the behavior will increase. Second is the idea of potency. The more potent or reinforcing the social reinforcer is, the greater the chances the reinforced behavior will occur again. Third is the notion of description. By describing to your child which of his behaviors resulted in your praise, desired learning will occur more rapidly.

One advantage of using social reinforcement is that it is easy to do so. Praise, attention, affection, and recognition are available all the time. You don't have to go to the cupboard or department store to pick them up. You literally can use them when you catch your child doing something good. As soon as you see your child doing something that you would like repeated, praise or recognize the behavior as soon as possible after the behavior occurs. If your praise comes immediately after the behavior, you will see the behavior again. If there is an appreciable delay between behavior and your social reinforcement, you may not observe your desired outcome. This is particularly important with young children and extremely important with very young children. Your child's own verbal skills appears to be the strongest factor to consider when discussing this delay between behavior and the environmental reaction. For children who have little or no verbal behavior, there should be no delay whatsoever. For children who understand what you mean when you say, "I really want to thank you for cleaning up your room this morning," delay is tolerable. However, even with the older child, keep your delay to a minimum. The reasons are simple. During the delay period, other behaviors may take place that might cause you to withhold your social reinforcement, or your child might say to himself, "I finally make my bed, and no one even cares." Adults also have difficulty in handling delays. Sometimes the phone call, 3 weeks after the dinner party, doesn't do the trick. Try the best you can to offer your attention as close to the behavior as possible. A simple word of thanks, an affectionate pat on the head, or a warm smile offered immediately upon observing a behavior you see as desirable can make your day a lot easier.

Unfortunately, there is no guarantee that our words of praise and recognition will be reinforcing. This brings us to the idea of potency. Social reinforcers obtain and maintain their potency because they are occasionally associated with other types of reinforcers such as food, movies, toys, and candy. Each time you associate yourself or your words of praise with a toy, special dessert, or trip to the zoo, you are helping to maintain the effectiveness of your attention and recognition. The effect comes about automatically. Each time you warmly kiss your child, hug him, or tickle his ribs, you are again maintaining the reinforcing properties of your words and actions.

Finally, keep in mind the idea of describing to your child which of his behaviors were particularly pleasing to you. For example, saying to your child, "Thanks, hon, for *putting your toys away*—that helps me a lot," will be much more effective than just telling him that he is a good boy. Make it easy for him to know what you would like for him to do again in the near future.

WATCH THE BEHAVIORS YOU ARE ATTENDING TO

Just about every parent, including myself, has at one time or another socially reinforced a behavior without meaning to increase it. If we do not watch what we are attending to that behavior will end up on our not-so-good list. The term excessive has to be introduced, and you have to be the one who determines what excessive means to you. If, for example, our child is riding a new rocking horse and in the excitement she falls off and begins to cry, we are going to run over to see if she is hurt. We might pick her up, tell her everything is all right and, if she asks, put her right back on. Technically, our child has received social reinforcement—our attention—during and after crying. By our actions, we have increased the possibility of seeing the crying again. Quite honestly, most parents do not give that possibility a second thought, and that is how it should be. It is much more important to let your child know that she should come to you when she is hurt than to worry about the possible effects of your attention. However, what you must keep in mind is that if your child's crying becomes the *predominate* means for her to gain your attention, you are going to have to deal with excessive crying. A child must know that his parents will listen, understand, and try to help when he is not feeling well, or is crying, or is upset. Parents' understanding and caring are as important as any statement of praise or recognition. But make certain that those times are not the only times when he receives your understanding, caring, and affection.

"GRANDMA'S RULE"

A second approach for increasing behavior is called Grandma's Rule. It is an approach that you have used many times. The reinforcer, instead of being praise, is usually a game, activity, or special treat. In his book,[3] *Parents are Teachers*, Dr. Wesley Becker has listed several examples of familiar Grandma's Rules:

"You can go play ball when you finish your homework."

"When everybody is seated at the table and quiet, Father will say Grace and we can eat."

"Eat your vegetables and then you can have some pie."

"When your room is picked up, I've got a special treat for you."

"Take your bath and then you can have some cookies and milk."

"You can go out and play after you take out the trash."

Notice in these examples that a specific behavior must occur first; it is then followed by something the child wishes—homework is required before playing ball, and pie is withheld until the child eats his vegetables.

One of the advantages of this approach is that the present reinforcer is evident from the child's own behavior. What the child would like to do or have at the moment is the reinforcer you can use to have the child do what you consider to be appropriate. A second advantage of Grandma's Rule is that communication between parent and child is

[3]W. C. Becker, *Parents Are Teachers: A Child Management Program*, Champaign, Ill.: Research Press, 1971, p. 24.

usually very clear and understandable. The child is informed that as soon as he makes his bed, he can watch television. The desired behavior is clear, and the environmental reaction is equally clear. A third major advantage of this approach is its positive nature. The child knows what will happen when he accomplishes the task instead of being told what will happen if he *doesn't* do the task. From Dr. Becker's book:[4]

Justin's Mother Learns To Use Grandma's Rule

At first, Mother told Justin, "You didn't make your bed so you can't go out and play." Justin pouted all day and still did not make his bed. He said, "Why should I? I can't go out and play anyway . . . ."

Justin's mother then heard about Grandma's Rule and the importance of reinforcers. She told Justin, "When you make your bed, you can go out and play." Justin lit up. "You mean I can go out if I make my bed? Yippie!" The bed was made in 2 minutes, and Mother was able to praise and hug Justin for doing a good job.

All the advantages of Grandma's Rule are beautifully depicted in this simple episode. First, the reinforcer for Justin was apparent. He wanted to go outside to play. What Mother wanted was equally apparent. Second, communication between Justin and his mother was clear and precise—when you make your bed you can go out and play. Third, Mother's approach changed from the negative to the positive. Justin was told how his environment would react to him when he completed the desired task. Finally, an advantage not mentioned before—it worked! Both Mother and Justin were pleased about that.

USING GRANDMA'S RULE EFFECTIVELY

This approach is easy and effective if you will keep the following points in mind. First, there must be a potent reinforcer for Grandma's Rule to work. By watching or listening to your child, you should be able to find a good reinforcer. Remember, there may be a big difference between telling your child that you will take him bowling once his room is cleaned and telling him that when he cleans up his room he can have a bowl of spinach. In the second case, room cleaning will only occur if Popeye is one of the child's heros. For that matter, room cleaning will occur only if bowling is desired by the child.

Second, with very few exceptions, the reinforcer must be given only

[4] Ibid., p. 26.

after the desired behavior has taken place. The exception to this would be if the child not only assures you he will complete the task, but that *he does* complete the task as promised. Many of us allow our child to go to the movies when he tells us he will finish his homework when he returns. There is nothing wrong with this as long as the homework is, in fact, finished at the time promised. However, if the child fails to complete his end of the bargain, the reinforcer should no longer be offered first in the near future. Point out why the restriction is being imposed and require several "behaviors first" before allowing the reinforcer to again come before the behavior. If you will be consistent in this respect, your child will learn he must keep his promise or otherwise lose the privilege of having the reinforcer first.

Skiing Before Homework

At nine years of age, Jerry was already an accomplished skier. He, however, was not an expert at doing homework. During the winter months, Jerry could almost always be found on the slopes. His mother and father were present at an inservice I provided for parents and, after hearing about Grandma's Rule, they decided to try it. Homework was the desired behavior, and skiing was to be the reinforcer. I received a call from the mother about two weeks after my presentation. After talking for a few moments, she politely stated, "I thought you said this approach works." I answered that in many cases it does—but not always.

She described what she was doing and, in a short time, the difficulty became apparent. First, the reinforcer had to be delayed as a result of skiing occurring only on the weekends. Second, Mother indicated she hadn't been very consistent. Of the three weekends that had passed since the presentation, Jerry was allowed to go skiing even though he had only done his homework a few days during one week. As such, Jerry soon realized he was going to be allowed to go skiing whether or not he did his homework.

In order to accomplish the homework goal, the following program was started. The parents were to take Jerry skiing the next weekend regardless of whether the homework was completed. During the two days of skiing, the parents were asked to count the number of "runs" Jerry made during each day. (A run is skiing from the "top" to the "bottom" of the mountain slope.) Jerry was not told that his parents were counting the runs, and no limitations were placed on the number—he could ski for as long as his legs held out. On Saturday, Jerry made 10 runs and, on Sunday, he made 9. When the family returned home Sunday evening, the following information was given to Jerry.

For each night Jerry did his homework correctly and completely, he earned two runs. When he did his homework correctly during every school night, he earned unlimited runs for the upcoming weekend. (Homework completed for four nights = eight runs; homework completed all five nights = unlimited runs.) A chart was set up in Jerry's room and he was asked to mark down whether he had completed his homework and how many runs he had earned. The program was clearly explained to Jerry. He was urged in a positive way, to do his homework so he could go skiing. He was told by his parents that they were going to stick with the program, and they did. Their son's homework problem was solved. During the nonwinter months, other reinforcers were established, and the desired homework behavior continued.

One of the problems with Jerry's parents initial approach was the delay between homework accomplished early in the week and the reinforcer being withheld until the weekend. This type of delay is sometimes inevitable. Whenever possible, the reinforcer should be given immediately after the desired behavior has occurred. This is particularly important when you first begin to use Grandma's Rule. It is necessary to show your child that his desired behavior will be recognized. In Jerry's case, the chart with the marks and earned runs helped to bridge the gap between the delay of work and reinforcement. Additionally, Jerry's parents were urged to use much social reinforcement for completed homework, which also helped to bridge this gap. I talked with Jerry's parents several months later. Mother told me that Jerry had decided that he no longer needed the chart; he would remember to do his homework on his own. She also told me that one of his new fifth-grade teachers had gotten him very interested in astronomy and he wasn't skiing as often, but he was still doing his homework.

Both sides of Grandma's Rule must be made clear to the child. He must know what the desired behavior is and what the reinforcer will be. Our children do not always know what we expect of them. We need to communicate clearly and precisely. "When you clean up your room, we will go bowling" is not as clear as saying, "When you put your shoes away, hang up your coat, and your bed is made, we will go bowling."

When Grandma's Rule is used, both parties must comply with what has been agreed on. I have already mentioned that the child must do his part, otherwise the reinforcer is withheld. The parent must also do the same. When the desired behavior has been accomplished, the agreed on reinforcer must be given. Frustration, confusion, and most certainly a decrease in desirable behavior will occur when an agreed on reinforcer is withheld when a child has satisfactorily accomplished what was asked of him.

TOKEN SYSTEMS

Many parents have experienced a great deal of success in increasing different behaviors through the use of an approach called a token system. Basically, a token system is a method by which children earn points for desired behavior. Eventually, the points are exchanged for some type of material reinforcer. Some of the teachers you had in elementary school used a token system to reinforce your behavior when you were a student. During spelling period, for example, one of my teachers would place a gold star by each student's name after he had correctly spelled five words. Once we had collected 10 stars, we were given 15 minutes of free time to read magazines, work puzzles, or just sit around and quietly talk with one another. Her approach made spelling class very enjoyable, and we also learned a lot.

Randy and Bed-Wetting

At six and one-half years of age, Randy was still wetting his bed about five times each week. His parents had tried many different approaches to stop the behavior, but they had no success. At one point, all liquids were withheld for three hours prior to bedtime, but he still wet. They also required that he wash his sheets in the bath tub, but that didn't work. Sometimes they would wake him up around ten o'clock to go to the bathroom, but even then he would wet sometime later. They verbally "punished" him by telling him that only babies wet their beds and big boys don't, but that just upset the parents.

During the first meeting with Randy's parents, I asked them if the family doctor had been consulted. They said yes. Apparently, the physician found no physical reason for the child's bed-wetting. I asked the parents if there was anything really special that Randy liked to do, and I was told he enjoyed assembling plastic model cars. The parents were asked if they would be willing to use the model cars as reinforcement, and they agreed. The following token system was established for Randy. After being discussed with his parents, Randy and I sat for a few minutes alone so I could explain the system to him.

First, the parents were urged to no longer use the terms of baby and big boy as a means of punishment. Instead, no comment whatsoever was to be made when the child wet his bed. This suggestion was made for two reasons. On the one hand, the parents' attention might be socially reinforcing, therefore helping to maintain the bed-wetting. On the other hand, the token system itself, coupled with considerable social reinforcement for nonbed-wetting should be relied on to bring about the desired change.

Second, a brightly colored chart was placed in Randy's room. The chart had Randy's name printed on the top and the days of the week (four weeks) printed in one-inch blocks on the remainder of the chart. Randy was given two small boxes of stars that he was to keep in his dresser. One box contained gold stars, the other blue ones. A small, empty jar was also given to Randy. The jar was to be his bank. It was selected so he could see how much he had earned.

Each blue star would be worth 10 cents and each gold star would be worth 5 cents. When Randy had a dry night, a blue star would be placed in the appropriate block and a dime would be placed in his bank. When there were consecutive dry nights, a gold star was placed in the appropriate block and a nickel bonus was placed in the jar. (For example, if he was dry the first night of the program, he received a blue star and a dime. If he was also dry on the second night, he received a blue and gold bonus star and 15 cents. If he wet on the third night, he received nothing. If he was dry on the fourth night, he was given a blue star and a dime. For each additional consecutive dry night, he received two stars—one blue, one gold—and 15 cents.)

Randy was allowed to spend his earnings anytime and anyway he wished. Since he really enjoyed building model cars, it was suggested that he save some of his earnings so he could go to the store with his mother and purchase one of the models. Whenever he was given a star, both Father and Mother socially reinforced the dry behavior enthusiastically and warmly.

Randy wet his bed the first night, but nothing was said about it the following morning. (Mother told me that she probably had a disappointed look on her face.) He was dry the second night, and he received the blue star—which he himself put up—a dime, and a lot of praise from his parents. His mother was so pleased that she praised him throughout the entire day. In fact, she called me twice to tell me about it. Unfortunately, her enthusiasm was a little premature, for Randy wet the following night. It took about two weeks before his wetting began to consistently decrease. During a three-month follow-up meeting, the parents indicated that Randy had had only two wet nights. The token system was maintained for an additional month. Afterwards, being dry and being occasionally praised by his parents was enough reinforcement for Randy.

One of the advantages of a token system is that the child is continually aware of his own progress. By looking at *his* chart and *his* stars or points, he can see how well he is doing. The stars also help to bridge the gap between desired behavior and material reinforcers (in about the same way our paychecks bridge the gap between our work and our own reinforcers).

One of our goals as parents is to teach our children to learn how to get used to delays, for the older a child becomes, the longer he usually has to wait for his reinforcement. Token systems are one way to help teach how delay in reinforcement works. The points and stars actually become a form of reinforcement, and children begin to work hard to accumulate the stars. Eventually, the stars are replaced by the parents' social reinforcement, at which point a token system is no longer needed to teach and maintain desired behavior.

Jenny and Coming Home When Called

Jenny's mother was about to go "through the roof." She would often spend over a half-hour getting Jenny to come inside the house when it was dark. Usually, five or six requests (eventually demands) were required before Jenny would come bouncing home. Neither Mother nor Father wished to punish their daughter for not minding because she was having such a good time with her friends. But Mother's frustration about Jenny's not coming in had reached a point where the parents decided something needed to be done.

Jenny enjoyed television. However, she was not allowed to watch it on school nights. She could watch it on weekends, but only on a limited basis. Jenny's parents were asked if they would be willing to use television time on weekends as a reinforcer for teaching Jenny to come home when first called. They agreed, and the following program was developed and explained to Jenny.

Jenny would be able to earn extra weekend television time by coming home when first called. For each school night when she came home right away, she would earn 10 extra minutes of TV. However, if she failed to come in on time, she would lose five minutes. If there were two consecutive nights of not coming when called, an additional five-minute penalty was established.

A chart was placed in Jenny's room. Her name and "Extra TV time" were printed on the top and the days of the week (four weeks) made up the remainder of the chart. Jenny was given two boxes. One contained gold stars and the other small black "X's" Mother cut out from black poster paper. Each evening Jenny came in on time, she placed a star in the appropriate block. If she failed to come in she would have to place an "X" in the block. If she failed to come in for two straight nights, she would have to place two "X's" in one block.

Jenny's mother was asked to give her daughter a 15-minute signal when she was outside playing. For the first few evenings of the program, Mother was asked to remind Jenny of the television token system. When the 15 minutes had transpired, Jenny's mother was to call her daughter into the house. When Jenny came home within 10 minutes, she earned a gold star. If she came home after that time, she earned her "X."

The program worked very quickly. Her parents were flexible in regard to the 10-minute period; sometimes they would extend it several minutes without Jenny knowing about the extension. Each time Jenny came home when first called, her parents gave their daughter much praise. The praise was directly related to coming home instead of just to Jenny—"You are such a good girl for coming home on time. Let's go put your star on your chart." (This social reinforcement was very important, for it is the base on which the token system can be removed.)

After three weeks of the token system, the parents were shown how to gradually remove it. For the first four days of the week (Sunday through Wednesday), the stars were still used. On Thursday, when Jenny came in within the 10-minute period, she was told she did not have to place a star on her chart if she didn't want to, for her parents were very pleased and they would remember that she had earned her extra time. On Friday, before dinner, Jenny's parents told her she had earned one hour of extra TV time because she had come home all five school nights. This social reinforcement made the Thursday night star unnecessary. During the following week, stars were no longer given for Wednesday or Thursday, but were replaced by praise and attention. By the end of the following week, the token system was no longer needed. Jenny now received a good deal of social praise for coming home when called, as well as her extra TV time. In the event that Jenny did not come in when called, the loss of TV time was still used, but the "X" was no longer placed on the chart.

PENALTY POINTS AND TOKEN SYSTEMS

There is some disagreement among behavioral psychologists as to whether penalties or minus points are necessary in a token system. This disagreement has not been totally resolved. In my experience, I have found that the penalty side of a token system is not only helpful, but at times necessary. However, when minus points are employed, it is necessary to watch very carefully how we are responding to our child. Otherwise, *we* may accidentally be responsible for some of our child's minus points or penalties.

Mark and Going to Bed on Time

Bedtime was not Mark's favorite time. He could come up with 10 different reasons and requests for delaying the inevitable. In most cases, he was quite successful in postponing bedtime for a minimum of a half-hour. Unknowingly, his parents had taught him these delaying tactics; not only were they excellent teachers, Mark was a quick learner. Since Mark enjoyed staying up as long as possible, extra stay-up time on the weekends seemed to be a perfect reinforcer.

After discussing a token system approach with Mark's parents, they agreed to allow their son one extra hour of stay-up time on the weekends. The one hour would be divided in any way Mark decided between Friday and Saturday nights. His parents believed that by having their son make the decision about the extra time, he would begin to learn something about responsibility and learn to manage his own reinforcement.

The program was relatively simple. Mark was given a 30-minute signal that bedtime was coming. When the 30-minute period was up, he was to go to bed and his parents would come in and kiss him goodnight. When he went to bed as requested, he earned 12 minutes of extra stay-up time. If he failed to go to bed immediately, he would not earn any extra time. At the parents' request, no minus time was to be used when Mark failed to go to bed on time.

A blue marking pen was used to keep track of the earned time. Mark would color in a block on his chart the following morning when he went to bed on time the night before. The reason for the delayed marking was to avoid the situation where he would have already marked the chart and then gotten up out of bed.

The program went fairly well during the first two weeks. Mark went to bed three of the five school nights during the two weeks without any difficulty. One problem, however, was noticed. Thursday night of the second week, Mark put up quite a fuss. Bedtime was delayed for almost an hour. But since he had gone to bed on time for three previous evenings, he had earned a little over a half-hour, which could have been used for Friday evening if Mark chose to do so. His parents quickly realized that Mark could earn this half-hour period of time and still demonstrate some fairly disruptive bedtime behavior twice a week. When I again suggested that penalty time be added to the token system, they reluctantly agreed to try it for two weeks. Mark was told that for each night he went to bed on time, he would earn his 12 minutes and a blue mark. However, if he did not go to bed as requested, he would have to give himself a blue "X" and lose 15 minutes of stay-up time. As one might expect, Mark did not like this addition. He was told several times that he would *never* have to lose these 15 minutes if he would go to bed when asked.

During the first week of this additional program, Mark went to bed on time four of the five nights and earned 33 minutes of extra bedtime. He used all 33 minutes on Friday evening, which left him no extra time for Saturday night. He did not put up a fuss, because he realized that by doing so, he would lose more time for the following weekend.

During the second week, he once again went to bed four of the five school nights. Although his parents were pleased, I decided to chat with them to see if something they were doing might be responsible for the one night failure.

From our discussion, the following was disclosed. First, the parents were still giving Mark his 30-minute warning. Second, the parents made certain that during those 30 minutes, Mark would remain relatively quiet—no wrestling or running around the house. Third, the parents agreed that they were having a hard time maintaining some consistency in regards to Mark's bedtime requests—water, tissue, or going to the bathroom. For both of the failure nights, Mark would begin to make requests after he had gone to bed on time. This usually resulted in an extra 10 or 15 minutes of staying up. His mother, in turn, would warn him several times that if he was not back in bed immediately, he would lose 15 minutes for the weekend.

The parents were asked to keep giving the 30-minute signal; to continue to have quiet games during the 30 minutes; and to make certain that Mark be given every opportunity for his bedtime requests, but he should have them during the 30-minute period. Once in bed, no other requests would be granted unless a serious problem came up. His parents were no longer to remind him of the 15-minute penalty. Their reminders were attention given when he was not in bed. As such, his parents might be accidentally maintaining not only his delaying tactics, but also his penalty. Finally, when Mark awoke the following morning and had gone to bed when requested the previous evening, his parents were to praise his behavior while he placed a blue mark on his chart.

Thereafter, bedtime was rarely a problem.

Whenever you use minus points in a token system, you must be very careful that your social reinforcement is not maintaining the very behavior you are going to penalize your child for. In a sentence, it simply is not fair.

BEHAVIOR PAIRS: A FIRST LOOK

In both Mark and Jenny's case we were actually working with two behaviors, not just one. For Mark, the two behaviors were going to bed on time and *not* going to bed on time—or delaying tactics. For Jenny, the behaviors were coming in when called and *not* coming in on time.

Earlier I suggested that many of us have fallen into the habit of responding to our children when they do something that doesn't particularly please us, while *not* responding to them when their behavior is much more desirable. One way for us to help ourselves out of this habit is to keep in mind that every undesired behavior has a more desired opposite partner. For example, a child cannot be sitting in his chair at the same time he is out of his chair. Sitting and being out of a chair are incompatible opposite behaviors. A child cannot walk in the house and run in the house at the same time. I call these sets of incompatible behaviors behavior pairs. A behavior pair is a set of two behaviors—one that is desirable and one that is not so desirable. Although we will look extensively at behavior pairs when we talk about punishment, let me show you how they are used in complex (as well as simple) token systems.

Eddie and a Whole Host of Problems

Eddie's name was first mentioned to me during a conversation with a principal of an elementary school for which I was a consultant. Eddie's mother had contacted her in hopes of obtaining some professional help for her son. The principal was perplexed by the mother's concern, since Eddie had always been well behaved in school and had at least average grades. That afternoon I spoke with Eddie's mother and set up a time to discuss the situation. Before talking with the parents, however, I wanted to observe Eddie in his classroom.

Initial observation of this 10-year-old failed to reveal anything unusual. With the exception of a little talking to a neighbor when the teacher's back was turned toward the class, his behavior seemed to be fine. A brief question and answer period followed a writing assignment; Eddie answered some questions and was not at all disruptive. Several additional observation periods over the next three days proved equally uneventful.

The parents and I sat in their living room discussing my recent observations. Both parents appeared surprised at my description of their son's behavior. "Maybe we should leave him in school all day," Father suggested with an audible chuckle. "How can a child be so good at school and so bad at home?" he asked. Then he quickly added, "He really isn't that bad, it's just so many little things that cause his mother and me problems. I guess he is no different than most boys his age."

I asked the parents to describe some of the behaviors that were creating some difficulty. They came up with the following:

1. Not getting dressed on time before breakfast.
2. Not doing his homework.
3. Not following parents' requests.
4. Not eating his dinner.
5. Not going to bed on time.
6. Never helping with the chores.
7. Leaving soiled clothes on bedroom floor.

Once the above list was completed, the parents and I began to establish the behavior pairs. Each desired opposite behavior was carefully written so as to make communication between the parents and Eddie very clear. The following were the alternative behaviors—the behaviors to be increased.

1. Being dressed by 7:30 a.m. on school days.
2. Homework.
   a. Doing it without being asked.
   b. Being asked once.
   c. Being asked twice.
3. Following Mom's or Dad's request.
4. Finishing food on plate.
5. Going to bed by 8:30 p.m. on school nights.
6. Chores.
   a. Helping wash dinner dishes.
   b. Taking out garbage.
   c. Mowing lawn.
   d. Feeding the dog at 6:00 p.m.
7. Placing soiled clothes in clothes hamper as soon as they are taken off.

Instead of relying on one reinforcer to be used with so many different behaviors, several reinforcers would be made available to Eddie. Eddie was asked to give us some suggestions as to what he would like to work for, and he was happy to help us. The parents took Eddie's list and, along with their own, a reinforcement menu was developed.

1. Piece of candy.
2. Extra television time.
3. Going to a movie.
4. Eating dinner at a restaurant.
5. Fishing equipment—hooks, line, and sinkers.

6. Record album.
7. Having a friend sleep over.
8. Staying at a friend's house.
9. Money.
10. Staying up late on weekends.
11. Small toy.
12. A game of chess with Dad.
13. Special Dessert.
14. Going on a picnic with Mom and Dad.
15. Going fishing with Dad.
16. A new baseball glove or bat.

The parents' next task was to determine which of the above reinforcers were the easiest for them to give—the ones Eddie could have most often. The parents broke the reinforcers into two categories.

Easiest To Give	Most Difficult To Give
Candy	Movie
TV time	Eating out
Fishing equipment	Record album
Money	Friend over
Staying up late	Stay at friend's
Chess	Picnic
Dessert	Fishing with Dad
Small toy	Baseball glove or bat

The token system was almost complete. The next thing that had to be done was to assign point values to the behavior pairs. This was accomplished by asking the parents which of the listed behaviors were most critical to them. (Although I am presenting Eddie's complete token system to you, it did not start out this complex. During the first few weeks of the system, only three behaviors were worked with—going to bed on time, homework, and following requests. You will be much more successful with your token system if you will start out small—only a few behaviors to begin with. Otherwise, the system will be overwhelming to both you and your child and it is unlikely that either of you will continue with it.)

The parents agreed that bedtime, homework, and following requests were the most important behaviors. Therefore, greater point values were given to those behaviors. Getting dressed before breakfast was next, followed by eating all dinner food, helping with chores, and putting clothes away.

When we discussed assigning minus points, it was pointed out that minus points should be sufficient to deter undesired behavior, but they should not be so costly as to have Eddie end up with minus points for the day. In order for the token system to work, Eddie must end up with some plus points, since the only way he can earn reinforcement is to have a sufficient amount of plus points. The following points were assigned to the behavior pairs.

1. Going to bed on time	+ 10	1. Not going to bed
		   a. Asked twice −5
		   b. Asked three
		      times or
		      more −10

2. Homework
   a. Without being asked
   b. Asked once
   c. Asked twice
	+ 5
	+ 3
	+ 1
		2. Not doing home-
		   work −5

3. Following requests	+ 3
	(each
	time)
		3. Not following
		   requests
		   a. Asked twice −2
		   b. Asked three
		      times or
		      more −4

4. Getting dressed	+ 2	4. Not getting dressed −2

5. Chores
   a. Dishes
   b. Garbage
   c. Lawn
   d. Feeding dog
	+ 2
	+ 2
	+ 2
	+ 2
		5. Parents did not
		   want penalty
		   points for not
		   doing chores

6. Clothes in hamper (all soiled clothes must be put in hamper before plus points given)	+ 2	6. Clothes not in hamper −2
7. Eating dinner not included in token system—dealt with through Grandma's Rules		

(I can hear you saying that you need an accountant's degree to handle the bookkeeping, but it really isn't as bad as it initially looks.) Now we get to the last part of setting up the system. We have to assign points to the reinforcers on the menu. The parents were asked to estimate the *maximum* number of positive points Eddie would most likely earn per day if he did just about everything they desired. They came up with approximately 30 plus points (10 for bedtime; 5 for homework; 6 for requests—two requests per day; 2 for getting dressed; 4 for chores—two chores per day; and 2 for putting clothes away). Since it is necessary for Eddie to earn some reinforcement each day, some of the reinforcers must be very easy to obtain. This means that we must assign some of the reinforcers relatively few points. On the other hand, some of the reinforcers were expensive (baseball glove and record album) and some would require quite a bit of time on the part of the parents (picnic, fishing trip, and eating out). These reinforcers would require quite a few plus points before they could be earned. Before the plus points were assigned to the reinforcers, the parents were asked to determine how often they would realistically allow Eddie to have certain reinforcers. This is what they came up with.

1. Movie—once a month.
2. Eating out—once a month.
3. Record album—one every four months.
4. Friend stay over—twice a month.
5. Staying at a friend's house—twice a month.
6. Picnic—once every two months.
7. Fishing with Dad—once a month.
8. Baseball glove—on birthday (seven weeks away).

Since Eddie could earn approximately 30 points per day (210 points per week; 840-900 per month), points were assigned to the reinforcers on the basis of how often Eddie could have the reinforcer on a daily, weekly, or monthly basis. Eddie was told that certain reinforcers could be easily obtained, while others would require a little more work. He was told he could save his earned points and bank them in favor of a long-range reinforcer. He was also told he could only spend a maximum of 20 points per day and, once points were put in his bank, they would have to stay there until he had enough for one of the larger reinforcers. This was done so as to avoid the situation where he would spend previously earned points on a day where he had misbehaved and earned very few positive points.

Eddie's Token System	
Desired Behavior	**Undesired Behavior**
1. Going to bed on time + 10	1. Not going to bed on time −5, −10
2. Doing homework +5, +3, +1	2. Not doing homework −5
3. Following requests +3	3. Not following requests −2, −4
4. Getting dressed +2	4. Not getting dressed −2
5. Chores +2	5. Clothes not in hamper −2
6. Clothes in hamper +2	

Reinforcement Menu	
1. Candy +6 (maximum of three pieces)	7. Dessert +30
2. TV time +10 = 15 minutes (maximum ½ hour per day)	8. Small toy +150
	9. Movie +300 (one per month)
3. Fishing equipment +150 = 50¢ value	10. Eating out +300 (one per month)
4. Money +1 = 1¢ (maximum $1.50 per week)	11. Record album +2100
	12. Friend over +250
5. Staying up late +10 = 15 minutes (maximum ½ hour, weekend only)	13. Staying at friend's +250
	14. Picnic +1000
	15. Fishing with Dad +300 (one per month)
6. Chess +40 per game	16. Baseball glove and bat +800

Every effort was made to allow Eddie the opportunity to enjoy several different reinforcers. However, care was taken to insure that he received his reinforcers only *after* he had earned the necessary points. Slight exceptions were made to this last rule. If Eddie and his family decided to go out for dinner and Eddie was short a few points, his mother would find a way for him to earn the needed points. On one occasion he earned the extra points by reading one of his textbooks. On another occasion he earned extra points by helping his mother carry in the groceries. Mother carried a notebook with her so she could mark down the earned plus and minus points. Eddie could see the book anytime he desired and could see how much he had earned.

As noted, one of the reinforcers was dessert. This reinforcer was available only when Eddie ate all his dinner.

At the conclusion of every day, the plus and minus points were totaled, and the net positive points were determined. Eddie did not have to use any of his points; he could bank them if he chose to do so. In the initial days of the program, he was urged to spend some of his points so he could see how the token system worked.

According to Eddie's parents—who were the real judges—Eddie's program worked beautifully. Change for the better was noticed almost immediately. They found themselves using more social reinforcement with their son than ever before; his behavior made it easier for them to do so.

There were several other procedures used with Eddie and his family that I have not mentioned. For example, Eddie was given a half-hour signal that bedtime was coming. Very few requests were made of him during the first days of the program, and those that were made were very simple to carry out. He did not have to wash the dinner dishes, only help—usually by drying a few dishes or cleaning off some of the dinner table. Dressing himself in the morning was dealt with in a special way that I will describe in the next section. A clothes hamper was placed right by Eddie's bed to make it easier for him not to drop the clothes on the floor.

Every effort was made by Eddie's parents to guarantee success of the program. Their whole attitude was optimistic, warm, and affectionate. Any change or flexibility in the program was carefully explained to him.

It is hard to say what was responsible for the difficulties Eddie and his parents were having. There is no simple answer. The parents agreed that they were having a tough time being consistent with him. They described their situation as a kind of running snowball; as time passed things just gradually became worse. They told me that had they started much earlier, when Eddie was younger, to watch what they were doing, they wouldn't have had their present problems. When we first started talking, they realized that changes had to be made in order to bring some harmony and warmth to their family.

The token system was used for approximately four months. It was as much a benefit for the parents as for Eddie. It helped them to learn how to watch for Eddie's appropriate behavior. It helped them develop the habit of reinforcing Eddie for many small desirable actions. It helped them to discuss the types of behaviors they felt appropriate for Eddie, and it aided them in being consistent with what was agreed on. It was a very successful program.

REINFORCEMENT CAN WORK AGAINST YOU

Many of us accidentally increase the very behavior we wish to decrease through the incorrect use of social reinforcement. From *Changing*

Children's Behavior, John and Helen Krumboltz describe such an accidental situation.[5]

> "Binky was three-and-a-half years old but refused to dress himself. For several months his mother had been urging him to do so, but all her attempts had proved futile. 'Binky, please try to put on your shirt. I know you can do it. You are such a big boy. You can do so many other things. I know you can do this, too.' Binky refused to participate, and his mother eventually dressed him herself. The mother's coaxing did not convince Binky that he should dress himself. Eventually his mother stopped coaxing. She also stopped doing such a conscientious job of getting him dressed. One morning Binky came into the kitchen with his shirt on. Even though it was inside out his mother was delighted with his effort and let him know. The next morning he put his shoes on the wrong feet and without socks, but again his mother showed pleasure at his effort. From that point Binky made rapid progress in learning to dress himself."

As the Krumboltzes point out, coaxing is a form of attention and social reinforcement. Coaxing actually reinforces the opposite behavior of that which is desirable. Dr. Becker, in his book *Parents are Teachers*, offers another example dealing with the same behavior.[6] (Dr. Becker's approach was used with Eddie's dressing behavior.)

He reported that a parent decided it was time for her child to dress herself before going to school, allowing Mother time to prepare breakfast. The child, however, only partially dressed herself, and this resulted in the mother scolding the child. "Karen, what am I going to do with you? You'll be late for school. Now hurry up and get ready."

Five additional minutes did not alter the child's dressing. Once again, Mother responded. "Karen, come on, hurry up! You'll be late! Do I have to treat you like a baby?"

Dr. Becker analyzed the situation in the following way. When the child was put on her own to dress herself, Mother gave attention (scolding) only to the child's "dawdling." Not once did Mother praise Karen for getting herself partially dressed. What received immediate attention was *not* getting dressed. According to Dr. Becker, the child's mother had accidentally trained Karen to dawdle.

[5] Krumboltz, op cit., pp. 24-25.
[6] Becker, op cit., pp. 36-37.

Dr. Becker continued.

"Lisa's mother faced a similar task of helping her five-year-old to learn to get ready for school by herself. She too had over-babied Lisa by doing many things for Lisa that Lisa could have done by herself. When she realized the time had come, however, she approached it quite differently than Karen's mother.

First she told Lisa it was time for her to do more things for herself. The night before, she reminded Lisa about what she was to wear tomorrow, and together they set her clothes out where she could easily find them. When Mother woke Lisa in the morning Mother gave her a hug, and said, 'Let's see how far you can get dressing yourself while I put coffee on. I'll be right back to check.' Lisa's mother was back within a minute and noted that Lisa already had her panties and slip on. She immediately commented on this. 'You really know how to dress yourself. That really pleases me. You're a big girl.'"

Both Karen's and Lisa's mothers were using social reinforcement, but they were not using it with the same behavior. As a result, one child dawdled, while the other learned to dress herself. The basic difference between each mother's approach was *when* their attention came.

Many of us have experienced giving in to a child's demands in a location where not giving in is difficult. Giving in will result in a very brief period of desired behavior but, in the long run, it almost always works against us.

Sally and the Supermarket

Sally and her mother were in a supermarket. Although only three years old, Sally had already learned that a crowded supermarket was *the* place to be persistent with her demands.

Sally's mother was divorced, and Sally had no brothers or sisters. Unless Mother could find a baby-sitter, she would take Sally along with her when she went to the store.

Sally's mother had fallen into the familiar trap of giving in to her daughter's demands only after the demands had reached an intolerable level. Mother would be placed in an embarrassing position when her daughter would begin to scream. To quiet her down, she would give Sally what she wanted—the reinforcer came while Sally was making her fuss.

Mother and I talked for a while, looking for possible solutions to this situation. These were the ideas we came up with.

1. When Sally screams, take her from the market and place her in the car, then return to the store to finish the shopping. This idea was rejected. Leaving the child alone in the car would be very unwise (and, I believe, illegal in some places).
2. Allow Sally to cry in the supermarket. Mother rejected this idea. She said she'd never make it!
3. When Sally screams, leave the groceries in the cart and take Sally home immediately. This idea was also rejected. Mother would be in the same situation she started with—no groceries.
4. Before walking into the supermarket, tell Sally that she will get a small surprise, but only if she is quiet. Mother agreed to try this.

The next time Mother took Sally to the store, Sally was told that when she was quiet for just a little while, Mother was going to give her a surprise. When Sally was quiet for a few minutes, she was given a half stick of gum. Sally was praised for helping Mother shop. The following time they went to the store, Mother waited for about five or six minutes of quiet behavior, then gave Sally the small piece of gum. She was again enthusiastically praised and thanked. However, on the third trip, a problem came up. Mother gave Sally a half stick of gum after she was quiet for about 10 minutes. The store was very crowded, and it took Mother much longer to do her shopping then she had anticipated. Sally was quite tired, and she was beginning to get irritable. Sally took the now well-used gum out of her mouth and innocently dropped it on the supermarket floor. Mother saw this, but realized that she had never told Sally that she wasn't supposed to do it. Before Mother could say anything, Sally asked—in a crying way—for another piece of gum. Mother knew that she was not going to give in to the crying request. On the other hand, she realized her daughter was not only very tired, but that she had also been very good for almost an hour. Without further hesitation, Mother drew her daughter's attention to a brightly colored floor display of a fruit drink. There was a mechanical giraffe whose head was moving back and forth. With a little bit of animated conversation about the giraffe's funny face, Mother was able to distract Sally, and her crying stopped. Mother kept the conversation going for about three minutes—during which time Sally was intently listening to her mother. After the three minutes, Mother said, "Sally, you have been such a good helper, and so quiet, would you like another piece of gum?" The supermarket problem rarely occurred again.

SUMMARY

Most children work very hard for their parents' words of praise and their expressed affection. I believe all parents honestly feel great pleasure when they do demonstrate their affection and praise. But there are times when our children do not do what we desire of them. When undesired behavior is frequent, it can be very difficult for a parent to demonstrate affection. Most certainly, the love for the child is still felt, but it is often difficult to give forth the love in the face of consistent and persistent misbehavior. If you are experiencing such a situation, consider the possibility of using small material reinforcers, or Grandma's Rule, or a simple or complex token system. By doing so, you give desired behavior a chance to occur. When it does occur, even just a little, there is a greater chance that you will begin to demonstrate your affection and warmth.

IS REINFORCEMENT BRIBERY?

Rewards and reinforcement presented after desirable behavior is *not* bribery! A paycheck given to you after your hard work is not bribery. When a teacher gives a child an "A" grade for excellent work, is she bribing him? No way! When your child says "DaDa" for the first time, and you ecstatically hug and kiss him and immediately repeat the sound back to him, is that bribery? I'd like to hear someone say yes to that!

Medals given for bravery; Oscars awarded for superb acting; a bowling trophy for a team's effort; a cub scout's first *earned* merit badge; these and other reinforcers are not forms of bribes. They are what they are meant to be—appreciation of accomplishment, of a job well done, of a desired behavior.

BUT SOMETIMES I JUST DON'T FEEL LIKE PRAISING HIM

The truth is that sometimes you and I just do not feel like praising our child when he has finally done something desirable. This is usually the case when we are quite upset with his misbehavior that has lasted for many minutes. When you experience such a situation, it is very important that you make every effort to respond to that desired behavior. Try not to let it go unrecognized; otherwise, you are probably going to see a continuation of the misbehavior. "But won't my child realize that I am not being as sincere as I am most of the time?" That's the question most often raised when I make the above suggestion.

A child can pick up differences in the way you respond. A gruff "thank you" will come across much different than a pleasant, animated "thank you," particularly if you are rarely gruff. As hard as it may be for you, *don't* be gruff! Even if your mood "prevents" you from really meaning it, take a deep breath and warmly praise his behavior as you usually do. He will "see through you" only if *your* behavior is different than what he is accustomed to. You, of course, can say to yourself (or to your child), "I honestly do not feel like praising you, so I won't—even though you have just done something super." As noble as that may appear, it is going to work against both you *and* your child. *You* are just going to get deeper into your unpleasant mood, and *he* is going to come right down with you. Break the cycle by using whatever positive thinking devises you can—"Boy, am I going to feel better when he starts behaving desirably." Its amazing how quickly that warm, sincere feeling reappears when your youngster begins to behave appropriately. He will appreciate your praise and you will appreciate its effect.

Getting
Behavior
Started

It's November and there is an ad in the newspaper for an expensive and complicated toy that is on sale. I know my older son would love to have it. Once at the department store, I realize why there is such a big savings. I have to put the thing together. "Don't worry," the saleslady tells me, "a five-year old can follow the directions." When I hear that statement, I am reminded of a student who told me, "Nothing is impossible to the person who doesn't have to do it!"

Even though I know that I am going to regret it, I buy the 100 individual pieces that they call a toy. When I arrive home, I carefully open up the box and remove a crumpled piece of paper—the instructions. On the top of the page, in bold letters is written, "Don't worry about it, any five-year-old can follow these directions!"

Three days later the thing is together. That is, minus a few screws, nuts, and other things I can't even name. I know the manufacturer put those extras in there just to drive me and a lot of other people buggy. But the toy is together. According to the instructions, all I have to do is to push a small switch and the toy will begin to do all kinds of things. So I do. But it doesn't. It just sits there looking at me, and that's not what it's supposed to do. The instructions told me the toy will jump up and down, juggle three balls with one arm, and answer the telephone when it rings with the other arm. But it doesn't!

47

The decision I am left with is relatively simple. I can take it back to the friendly saleslady, or I can give it to my son before Christmas and let him put it together. I don't like either of those possibilities. I decide to ask my wife to take a shot at it. Not only does she find a spot for those "extras" I left out, but she also knows their names! When she's finished, the thing actually works. A most humbling experience.

REINFORCEMENT IS NOT ALWAYS ENOUGH

My problem is that I simply have never had a great deal of instruction or experience with putting such things as nuts, bolts, and screws together. Unless the instruction's pictures are very clear, I am in trouble. If I can't understand what I need to understand in order to accomplish the task, I am going to have a very difficult time getting the job done. And understánding, in part, is dependent on how much experience and teaching I have had.

Up to this point of the book, I have discussed positive reinforcement. Although reinforcement is critical, it isn't always enough. In fact, all the reinforcement in the world will not teach a child certain skills or behaviors unless he, too, has had sufficient experience and instruction.

BE SATISFIED WITH A LITTLE AT FIRST

In some instances, parents expect too much from their children. They often withhold reinforcement from their child until he behaves precisely as they wish. Since the child may not have the necessary skills to do what his parents desire, the result may be that neither the parent nor the child gains much from the experience. Instead of waiting for a desired behavior to take place *in toto*, you should reinforce gradual improvements and gradual performance that eventually lead to the total desired behavior.

From *Changing Children's Behavior,*[7]

Making One's Own Bed

Six-year-old Polly had never before attempted to make her own bed. One day she pulled up the blanket on the bed. Her mother told her that her bed looked nice. The next day Polly pulled the blanket and also straightened her pillow. Again her mother noticed the improvement. On successive days Polly began pulling up the sheet along with the blanket

[7] Krumboltz, op cit., p. 37.

and finally the bedspread. Although the bed would not pass military inspection, it represented a substantial improvement for Polly, and her mother expressed her appreciation.

What is most apparent in this example is that Polly's mother did not wait for Polly to do a perfect job before she reinforced her daughter's efforts. Instead, Polly was reinforced for gradual improvement.

Jimmy and His Toys

After being told 12 times, Jimmy finally realized his mother wanted him to put his toys away. So he did, but he squashed them underneath his bed. Mother probably wouldn't have noticed right away had it not been for the leg of a stuffed bear that didn't quite make it under the bedspread. Mother told Jimmy that she appreciated his efforts—it was some improvement—but she would prefer the toys to go in a toy box located at the foot of his bed. Three days after being asked, Jimmy put one of his toys in the box, and his mother showed him how happy she was. On the following day, four toys were found in the box, and again Mother showed her appreciation. Thereafter, Jimmy put most of his toys in the toy box.

Once again, reinforcement was given after gradual improvement. Had Mother waited for all the toys to be placed in the box before recognizing her son's efforts, she would have been putting the toys away for some time to come.

WHO MAKES THE FIRST MOVE

There is a noticeable problem with both of these examples. Both Polly's mother and Jimmy's mother had to rely on their children's initial move. I suspect that there are plenty of Pollys and Jimmys who have yet to put the first toy away or make some move toward making a bed. Although recognizing and reinforcing gradual improvement is extremely helpful, you can do one of several things to get behavior started. First, of course, you can simply tell your child to make his bed or put his toy away. Sometimes that is all that's needed. More than likely, the bed will only be partially made, and only a few toys will be put away. Even so, that is when reinforcing gradual improvement is absolutely essential. If you do tell your child to do something and he accomplishes just a very small part of what you desired, it is effort on his part, and you should reinforce his behavior.

You can also go one step further. You can say to your child, "Today, we are going to learn how to make your bed." You can take one step of the task—pulling up the sheet—and model for your child what you want done. Again, the slightest effort on the child's part should be recognized. In this way, you do not have to wait for your child to make the first move, you make it. That is called modeling.

MODELING

When I was small, I was "taught" to swim by a method that wasn't too creative. The instructor would throw my friends and me into the lake and hold a long bamboo pole just beyond our reach. We either made it to the pole or we made it to the bottom of the lake. The instructor was always fond of saying that he never "lost" one of his pupils. His record may have been true, but his "sink or swim" method certainly took the fun out of the activity. His approach also kept many of us away from the water for a long time. He didn't believe in modeling or showing us what to do, and he most certainly did not believe in the gradual improvement approach. For him, it was all or nothing!

Betty and Swimming

Betty's parents had recently moved to Florida, and the home they had purchased had a lovely pool. Betty was five years old, and her parents wanted to teach her to respect the water and learn to swim. Her mother was a student in one of my classes and, for her class project, she decided to teach Betty to swim the length of the pool (about 45 feet).

Mother took Betty by the hand. They walked down the steps of the pool and sat down on the third step. The water was up to Betty's stomach. They sat for a few minutes splashing around. Betty laughed and threw water all over her mother and herself. Then Mother walked into the pool and started to swim for a moment or two. Betty was asked if she would like to hold on to her mother and take a ride in the water. This was done for about two minutes, and then Betty was placed back on the steps. Mother did not want to move too quickly. Soon Betty asked if she could ride again. Mother praised her daughter's enthusiasm and happily took her for another ride. Mother took Betty over to the wall in the shallow end of the pool and showed her daughter how to hold on to the wall. After a few moments, Mother began to kick her feet while holding on to the wall. Almost immediately, Betty started to imitate what her mother was doing. She was warmly praised.

On the following day, Mother and Betty repeated the previously practiced sequence. Afterward, Mother told Betty to watch while she put her face in the water and blew some bubbles. Again, Betty followed her mother's example. This was the first time Betty ever put her face completely under water. Blowing bubbles was apparently reinforcing in itself, for Betty played that way for almost an hour. During the next three days, Mother showed Betty how to float, move her arms, and kick her legs while keeping them straight. Each step was practiced until Betty was quite proficient. Mother showed Betty that by floating, kicking, and moving her arms, she could move through the water. Each time Betty progressed a little farther, Mother gave her lots of praise. When Betty's father came home in the evening, she would show him how well she was doing. Within two weeks, Betty was not only swimming the length of the pool, but she was also learning how to dive. (I wish her mother would have been my teacher!)

Children can help their parents a great deal by serving as models for other children. For example, you can teach many desirable behaviors by having an older brother or sister help you in the teaching task. If an older sister is requested to keep her room straight and is praised for doing so, a younger sister might begin to imitate what she sees. This is more likely to happen if the older sister's behavior is expressly praised and she, in turn, shows her sister what it means to clean up a room.

MODELING CAN WORK AGAINST YOU

Parents, of course, are important models for their children. In most cases, what is modeled is desirable, but there are exceptions. Do you remember when the antismoking ads first appeared on television? One showed a father puffing away on three cigarettes while telling his son that it was dangerous to smoke and he didn't want him to do it. Good luck, Dad!   Follow through

The Hitter of the Neighborhood

There wasn't a day that hardly passed that Paul didn't punch one of the other children in the neighborhood. When someone started to cry you could predict that Paul was close by. Finally, one of the mothers on Paul's block went to Paul's mother to complain. "He's always been like that," Paul's mother explained. "I spank him everytime he hits someone. When he gets home, I'm really going to give it to him."

As soon as Paul did get home, his mother gave it to him. Paul's mother was doing the same thing to Paul as he was doing to the other children.

What's Good for Carol Is Good for Brother

Carol's parents decided to teach her not to play with the knobs on the television set. Their approach was straightforward—when Carol would touch the knob, her hand was slapped. It did not take many slaps for Carol to learn to avoid playing with the television set. Carol had a younger brother who was just beginning to walk. He thought the TV set would make a fine toy, so he began to play with the knobs. Carol quickly assumed the role of parent and, as soon as her brother touched the set, she would slap his hand. Her new role, however, did not stop there. Every time the brother would touch anything of Carol's he would receive a slap.

Undesired modeling is difficult to avoid, and the best we can do is to keep it to a minimum. If you see a sudden increase in a behavior that has not been observed before or not been observed for some time, look carefully at how you are reacting to other members of the family to see if you are setting up an undesired modeling situation. On the other hand, if your child has persistently engaged in a behavior that you do not approve of, see if someone in close proximity is setting the stage for the child's behavior.

DON'T GIVE UP TOO SOON ON "NEW" BEHAVIOR

Even with correct modeling and consistent reinforcement, there are times when we still fail to teach what we desire. Sometimes we ask too much of our children, considering their present age and ability. More times than not, however, we do not help them enough.

Terry and Her Bicycle

Terry's father was very concerned about his eight-year-old daughter's lack of athletic ability. He was paying so much attention to the "absence" of this ability that it was fast becoming a problem for both himself and his daughter. The basic difficulty centered around Terry's lack of interest in riding her new bicycle. She had fallen a few times and had found out that the easiest way to avoid falling was to avoid riding.

Up to a point, Terry's father had used a combination of modeling and the gradual reinforcement approach to teach his daughter to ride. He held the bike for her while she sat on it. He held on to the bike while running alongside, giving Terry a chance to steer the bike herself. He would let go of the bike every so often and show Terry that she was riding by herself. That is as far as he got. If he would let go for more than a few seconds, Terry and the bike would fall. She would complain about being hurt and he would become upset.

"She can't do it. She just doesn't have the coordination," Father told me.

The experience was not only frustrating to him, but painful to his daughter.

Terry's father sincerely believed that his daughter did not have the ability—coordination— to ride her bike. For me, he gave up just a little too quickly. We talked for some time. Although I agreed it was possible that he was correct, I suggested that instead of saying something was wrong with Terry (*her* absence of ability), perhaps something was missing in the teaching approach. Maybe Terry was not helped enough.

Somehow, Terry needed some assistance in order to move beyond the point of being on her own for a few seconds. On the following day, training wheels were purchased and attached to the back wheels of her bicycle. This would enable her to get the feel of a moving bike and experience some fun besides. A game was set up to see how far she would ride away and then back to her father. The training wheels also enabled Terry to ride at a fairly good speed—which is necessary to keep a bike upright. On the next day, Terry's father, with Terry watching, bent the training wheels ever so slightly away from the ground. Terry hopped on the bike and the game was repeated. After some practice, Terry was riding fast enough to maintain the upright position. However, if she did slow down, the training wheels would prevent the bike (and Terry) from falling over.

On the next day, Father showed Terry how to jump off the seat of the bike and land feet first on the ground. Before the training wheels were bent any further, this jumping-off activity was practiced until Terry was doing it without any difficulty. Then the wheels were bent further. Father stayed fairly close until Terry gained some speed. Within 15 minutes, she was riding all over the place. Father then removed the training wheels from the bike. Once again, he stayed close to his daughter until she was riding fast enough to keep the bike in a stable position.

She fell twice, but landed on her feet. With an "I'm Okay," she got back on the bike and rode some more.

You can help get behavior started by remembering several things. First, use a good deal of positive reinforcement for all initial correct performance, no matter how small the performance. Second, reinforce gradual improvements, again, no matter how small. Third, model for your child what you would like for him to do. Keep practicing what you have modeled until your child successfully demonstrates the modeled step several times. Fourth, once your child does a little bit of the desired behavior, move to a little more difficult and complex part of the total behavior. Fifth, if you get stuck, don't just stop. Ask yourself if you have helped your child enough. Maybe one small bridge will be just enough. Finally, be patient and show your child by your social reinforcement (and, if you wish, occasional material reinforcement) that you recognize his improved performance.

Keeping Behavior Going Once It Has Started

Success and self-confidence go hand in hand. By helping our child experience success, we can help him experience confidence. The more confidence he has, the greater the chances he will begin to explore and try new activities. It is because of these outcomes that initial reinforcement is so important. We contribute a great deal to our child's confidence by praising his early efforts, even when his first attempts only approximate the ultimate goal.

As ironic as it may first appear, however, research has shown that once a child begins to demonstrate a particular behavior consistently, we can help to maintain his success (or that behavior) by *not* reinforcing him each time the desired behavior occurs. We have learned that occasional and often unpredictable reinforcement is one of the best ways to keep behavior going once it has started. We can teach our child stick-to-it-iveness or persistence by showing him that his behavior will not always be praised. We can show him that by sticking to a task the chances for reinforcement increase.

When your behavior and mine occurs in the natural environment, it is almost always reinforced on an occasional or unpredictable basis, sometimes it comes and sometimes it doesn't. Cooking, for example, is rarely reinforced every time; some cookies turn out okay, while others flop! No teacher ever calls on a child every time he raises his hand, but only occasionally. Even Jack Nicklaus and Arnold Palmer "find" the sand on occasion. Sometimes our "blind" dates turn out to be just that. Sometimes the nickel we place in the Las Vegas slot machine turns into five dollars; other time it yields a lemon tree.

Even though our behavior is not reinforced every time, we still continue to bake cookies, raise our hands in class, play golf, and throw money into one-arm bandits. What accounts for our persistence and our stick-to-it-iveness? Occasional and unpredictable reinforcement seems the most plausible answer.

Dr. Wesley Becker, in his book *Parents are Teachers*, has offered several guidelines for parents when the questions of "when should I reinforce" and "how often should I reinforce" come up. Here is what he suggests.[8]

1. In teaching new tasks, reinforce immediately rather than permitting a delay between the response and reinforcement.
2. In the early stages of learning a task, reinforce every correct response. As the behavior becomes stronger, require more correct responses before reinforcing.
3. Reinforce improvement or steps in the right direction. Do not insist on perfect performance on the first try.

David and His Inactive Baseball Bat

David held the strike-out record for his second-grade baseball team. When it was his turn at bat, the outfielders would sit down on the ground and enjoy the sunshine. His physical education teacher tried to give him some reinforcement for his valiant attempts by having him dash off to first base whenever his bat would be fortunate enough to touch the oncoming ball. His classmates, however, weren't as considerate.

One of the main problems with David's swing was his eyes—he would close them just before he would swing the bat. David's father decided the time had come to help his son.

After showing David how to hold the bat and how to stand, Father presented David with a very large beach ball. The ball was rolled on the ground and David was asked to try to touch it with the bat when it came close to him. The first time the ball was touched, David's father could be heard from any location in the neighborhood praising his son's performance. David quickly learned that before he would be able to

[8] Becker, op cit., p. 35.

touch the beach ball consistently, he would have to watch it fairly closely.

Father's next step was to throw the beach ball in the general area of David's bat. David was told to hold the bat parallel to the ground and simply watch the ball. Everytime the ball hit the bat, Father shouted out his recognition. (Father did miss a few times, and I was not convinced that the missing was accidental.)

David was then shown how to swing the bat, while keeping his head reasonably still and his eyes opened. After several practice sessions, David could hit the beach ball almost everytime. Father, however, did not praise each hit. He began to comment on every other hit, then every third hit. Then he began to reinforce his son's performance only on an occasional basis.

During the next five practice sessions, Father introduced different size balls to David. Eventually, a softball was thrown. Each time a new ball was brought into the picture, Father reinforced every hit—no matter what the direction of the ball. After the hitting became fairly consistent, Father reinforced his son only occasionally.

Although David still struck out every once in awhile, the outfielders no longer sat on their duffs. David had learned how to give them a few surprises.

Once you begin to see that your child puts one toy away, or one soiled sock in the hamper on a fairly consistent basis, withhold your reinforcement until he puts two toys or both socks away. Gradually require a little more work before your praise and appreciation is offered. Be careful not to move too fast. Make certain that before you begin to decrease your reinforcement, your child's behavior—no matter how small— is occurring quite consistently.

Helping Jenny To Speak

Five-year-old Jenny had very few understandable words in her vocabulary. Although many physical examinations failed to pinpoint why she was not speaking, it was the general opinion of the examining physicians that Jenny was capable of speech. A program was undertaken by a qualified speech therapist to help Jenny acquire more vocabulary.

After about six hours of talking to and playing with Jenny, the speech therapist observed the following sounds and words: good-bye, aah, poppa, mm, and oou. There was some babbling and whining, but mostly there was silence.

Jenny was very fond of pretzels. She also appeared to enjoy people talking to her, particularly when the person who was talking was very animated.

The speech therapist's records indicated that Jenny would produce about one sound every 15 minutes. Because of this very low production, the therapist decided to reinforce any sound Jenny gave her.

Initially, the therapist attempted to model sounds for Jenny. When Jenny would repeat or echo what the therapist had said, Jenny would be given a piece of pretzel and lots of animated speech by the therapist. Ten days of the approach failed to bring about much change in Jenny's vocalizations. After talking with Jenny's parents, the therapist reluctantly decided to "wait" Jenny out. The therapist and Jenny sat together in a small room and the therapist said nothing until Jenny produced a sound. As soon as a sound was made, the therapist immediately and heavily reinforced Jenny. She gave Jenny a small piece of pretzel, and she echoed back to Jenny exactly the sound that Jenny had given her. Every single sound, no matter what it was, brought Jenny a great deal of hugging and animated conversation.

Within three one-hour sessions, Jenny began to give her therapist about 20 sounds every 15 minutes. At that point, the therapist began to wait for Jenny to give her two sounds before reinforcement was given. Jenny's vocalizations continued to increase. After one more hour, the therapist required that Jenny say three sounds before reinforcement. Within a short period of time, the number of sounds increased to about 200 in a 15-minute period.

The therapist decided to reintroduce the earlier modeling procedure. This time it was much more effective. The therapist would make a sound that Jenny had said many times. Because her procedure had changed, the therapist returned to reinforcing every correct echoed response which Jenny gave. After the echoing behavior began to occur consistently, the therapist began to require Jenny to work a little harder before reinforcement was given.

Soon, the therapist began teaching Jenny how to produce different sounds. They would practice teeth and tongue positions as well as different breathing exercises. Each time a new sound was introduced, the therapist reinforced every response. Then she would begin to require Jenny to come closer to the actual sound being modeled and practiced. Once the sound was produced accurately and consistently, the therapist again began to require a little more work from Jenny.

Speech therapy is still going on and will for some time to come. Jenny is making excellent progress.

There is one important point about the gradual reduction of positive reinforcement that needs mentioning. Be careful not to reduce too much of the reinforcement. If the amount of recognition we give becomes very limited, our child's behavior may come to an abrupt halt.

Alan and David and Their Room

The twins were four years old when their mother decided to teach them to keep their room in reasonable order. She began to watch for any attempt from either of the boys to put a toy away or put shoes or clothes in their closet. One evening, prior to bedtime, Alan placed one of his toys in the toy box. Mother told Alan how much she appreciated him putting his toys away—that it made things easier for her. David seemed to be listening, but he simply hopped into bed and said goodnight. The following afternoon, Mother noticed that David placed the same toy in the toy box. Again, she offered her thanks. That evening , each of the boys tried to put the same toy into the toy box. Mother suggested that if David wanted, he could put his tennis shoes in the closet, for this would make Mother very happy. As sometimes happens, a spurt of tidying behavior took place over the next three days. Thinking that her goal had been reached, Mother began to reduce the number of times she praised and thanked the boys. Although the tidying behavior continued, Mother failed to recognize her sons' efforts more than twice over the next three days. After a few more days of equally infrequent reinforcement the kids' toys, shoes, and clothes were once again deposited all over the room. Realizing that she had forgotten to call attention to her children's desired behavior, Mother began to reinforce them more often, and the cleaning up was once again established.

Our children's behavior is the best barometer we have to determine if we are moving too quickly or reinforcing too infrequently. Some children require very little reinforcement from us, while others require more, particularly in the very beginning of a new teaching program. In Alan's and David's case, Mother realized—after seeing that the boys' behavior had practically stopped—that she was reinforcing too infrequently.

Paul and His Attention Span

Paul's mother and his kindergarten teacher were very close friends. One evening, while having dinner together, the teacher asked Paul's mother if Paul ever stuck to a task when at home. Mother indicated she didn't think so, but that she honestly never gave it much thought. The teacher related that while at school, Paul rarely concentrated on a job or activity for any length of time. Even when it came time to cut, paste, and color—things the teacher "knew" Paul liked to do—he would only work for a very short period of time. He would just sit in his chair until the teacher came over to him to see if there was anything wrong. According to the teacher, Paul was beginning to sit more and work less.

* * *

After several conferences with the school psychologist, a program was developed to increase Paul's attention span at home and at school. Both Mother and Paul's teacher would follow the same program as closely as possible.

Paul was given several pieces of paper, some crayons, a scissors, and some glue. Mother provided a place for him to work in the family room at home. While at school, Paul, as usual, would work at his desk along with the rest of his friends. Both Mother and the teacher would wait for Paul to begin to work with his materials. He was asked to make anything he wanted. After approximately one minute of work, Mother or teacher would walk over to Paul. They would place one of their hands on his shoulder and briefly comment on how nice his work was. They would then walk away for a brief period of time. After another minute or so, they would return to Paul, once again praising his talents. Very gradually, they began to require a few more minutes of work before going over to Paul to recognize his creative endeavors. Within three days, Paul was sitting and working about the same amount of time as the rest of the children in his class.

After seeing how effective the School psychologist's program was, Paul's teacher began to use the same idea with all of the children in her room. She made a special point to reinforce each of the children occasionally for whatever task they were doing.

Again, a very gradual reinforcement approach was used to help Paul stick to his work. Before going on, I would like to see if you picked up on anything unusual from the above example. Reread the first paragraph, up to the three asterisks.

Behavior	Environment's Reaction	Results
Behavior 1 (Paul, sitting in his chair doing work)	Teacher's reaction *A* (very little attention— very little reinforcement)	*Decrease* in sitting in chair and *doing* work
Behavior 2 (Paul, sitting in his chair *not* doing his work)	Teacher's reaction *B* (more attention; "is anything wrong?")	*Increase* in sitting in chair and *not* doing his work
New Program		
Behavior 1 (Paul, sitting in his chair doing his work)	Teacher's reaction *C* (a good deal of praise and recognition for gradually more work)	*Increase* in sitting in chair and *doing* work
Behavior 2 (Paul, sitting in his chair *not* doing his work	Teacher's reaction *D* (little, if any, attention)	*Decrease* in sitting in chair and *not* doing his work

Did you recognize the possibility that Paul's teacher was accidentally reinforcing Paul when he was not working? Did you recognize the equal possibility that she had failed to give him much attention when he was doing his work? Once the teacher changed the way she responded to Paul's behavior, his behavior changed. Without realizing it, she, in part, may have been responsible for Paul's lack of work.

Let us look at another example of accidental reinforcement and the resulting accidental learning. Note that in this example, the parent is requiring that the child work a little harder—whine louder—before the reinforcement is given. Our example comes from Dr. Gerald Patterson's and Elizabeth Gullion's book, *Living with Children.*[9]

Sally, Her Toy, and Her Whining

Sally is playing with her brother. She wants the toy he is playing with. She whines and says, "Give me that toy." Her brother doesn't give her

[9] G. R. Patterson and M. E. Gullion, *Living With Children: New Methods for Parents and Teachers*, Champaign, Ill.: Research Press, 1968, p. 34.

the toy, so she whines louder. Mother gets upset about the noise and tells the brother to give Sally the toy. In this situation, Sally was being reinforced for whining. The reinforcer that Sally received was the toy . . . . Our prediction would be that in the future when things are not going the way Sally wants them to, she would whine.

Temporarily, Sally will stop her whining as a result of receiving the desired toy. In the long run, Mother has made things more difficult for herself, for she will undoubtedly hear Sally whine again. Suppose the next time Sally wants something, she fails to get it. She will probably start whining. Suppose further that Mother either doesn't hear the whining or decides to ignore it in the hopes it will stop. The result will be that Sally's protesting will increase; the whining either will grow more intense, or Sally will yank the toy from her brother. If the situation becomes annoying enough, Mother will step in and perhaps give Sally the toy. What Mother has accidentally done, by her reaction, is to require Sally to work a little harder—whine more or start yanking—before the reinforcer is given. Since she has required more work for the same amount of reinforcement (the toy), Sally's protesting will dramatically increase in the future.

Sara and Her Glass of Juice

Sara was sitting quietly watching "Sesame Street" on television. Her mother was in the kitchen baking some cookies. Sara asked Mother for a glass of juice, but Mother did not hear her daughter. After a few moments, Sara asked again. Mother was still occupied, so the juice was not given. Finally, the daughter raised her voice, and this time Mother gladly gave Sara the juice. Later that evening, a very similar situation took place. Only this time, Sara had to ask six times before she received what she wanted. As with the previous situation, Sara practically had to scream before she was attended to. Within a few days, Sara was doing something she had never done before—scream several times when she did not get what she wanted.

Without realizing it, Sara's mother began to reinforce her daughter after a request was made several times in a highly elevated tone. Notice that Sara had to work a little harder before getting her mother's attention.

Telling a parent that he must be very consistent in not rewarding undesirable behavior is like telling the dieter to stay away from beautiful chocolate candy; the advice is easy to give, while the not-doing is usually quite difficult. Nevertheless, the advice must be given. Without question, a major portion of my work with parents is helping them to avoid accidentally reinforcing undesired behavior, and particularly avoiding giving in to an undesired behavior that is already occurring at a fairly high rate. Dr. Becker offers us some advice—or cautions.[10]

1. *Caution.* If behavior is reinforced only now and then, it follows from what we know about intermittent reinforcement that such behaviors are likely to be persistent.
2. *Caution.* We can accidentally train our children into bad habits by occasionally giving in, even though we "know better." To change an undesirable behavior, the parent must be *very consistent* in not rewarding that behavior.

Before leaving this topic, let's see what can be done to help Sally's and Sara's mothers out of their situation.

Look at which of the children's behavior is receiving attention and what results from the attention.

Behavior	Environment's Reaction	Results
Behavior 1 (Sally, whining)	Mother's reaction *A* (attention and reinforcement—Sally receives the toy)	*Increase* in whining when Sally fails to get what she wants

Behavior	Environment's Reaction	Results
Behavior 1 (Sara, screaming)	Mother's reaction *A* (reinforcement—Sara receives her glass of juice and/or whatever else was wanted)	*Increase* in screaming when Sara is not attended to immediately or when she fails to get what she wants

[10] Becker, op cit., pp. 40-41.

We need to find out from the mothers what would be the desired alternative behaviors to the whining and screaming. Sally's mother indicates that she wants her daughter to play nicely with her brother—to share toys. Sara's mother tells us that she wants her daughter to ask for something politely. In addition, Sara's mother would prefer that her daughter come to her for what she wants instead of asking from another room. What reinforcement will be used? Sally's mother says she would like to use social reinforcement to increase the playing nicely, while Sara's mother says that she will use social reinforcement and whatever material reinforcer (juice, toy) Sara is asking for at the time.

	New Program (Sally)	
Behavior	Environment's Reaction	Results
Behavior 1 (Sally's whining)	Mother's reaction B (no reinforcement—toy is removed from Sally; Sally is removed from toy playing location and placed in a chair for two minutes of nonwhining, quiet behavior)	*Decrease* in whining
Behavior 2 (Sally's not whining and playing nicely with brother)	Mother's reaction C (a good deal of social reinforcement; Mother stops what she is doing and walks over to the children telling them how pleased she is that they are having such a good time playing together)	*Increase* in playing quietly with brother

New Program (Sara)		
Behavior	Environment's Reaction	Results
Behavior 1 (Sara's screaming)	Mother's reaction *B* (no reinforcement given when Sara screams for some object—juice is not given when Sara screams for it, toy is not given when Sara screams for it)	*Decrease* in screaming
Behavior 2 (Sara's asking politely for something)	Mother's reaction *C* (when mother decides that Sara may have what she requests the object—toy or juice—is given; much social reinforcement is given— "thank you for asking so nicely"; if Mother fails to hear Sara's quiet requests, Mother apologizes for not hearing, but tells her daughter that she should come to see Mother instead of raising her voice. Once Sara asks politely, the object is given)	*Increase* in asking politely for something

considerable reinforcement. Third, once you begin to see the desired
You may not wish to have Sally sit in a chair when she whines. There
are, of course, other ways to deal with the children's behaviors. But
there are three things that you should keep in mind regardless of the
approach you finally decide on. First, try to avoid reinforcing behaviors
that you consider to be undesirable. Second, make certain that all
initial appropriate behavior, no matter how infrequent or small, receives
behavior occurring more often, gradually reduce the frequency of your
reinforcement. Begin to require a little more desired behavior before
you offer your praise and attention.

Teaching Our Children What Not To Do

Unfortunately, too many of us spend a good deal of time doing just what the title suggests. Equally unfortunate is the observation that many of us aren't as successful as we would like to be when we attempt to teach our children what not to do. Ironically, it may be that our excessive effort decreases our effectiveness.

According to some psychologists, it is actually necessary to use certain punishing reactions or approaches before a child can learn what not to do. Dr. David Ausubel,[11] for example, has stated: "It is impossible for children to learn what is *not* approved and tolerated simply by generalizing in reverse from the approval they receive for the behavior that is acceptable." In essence, Dr. Ausubel is saying that simply because you reinforce your young child for playing with his toys does not mean he will learn to avoid playing with your expensive lamp. Dr. Harvey Clarizio[12] points out that "The use of punishment as an intervention technique is most likely necessary in that it is impossible to guide children effectively through the use of only positive reinforcement."

[11] D. Ausubel, "A New Look at Classroom Discipline." *Phi Delta Kappan*, 1961, *43*, pp. 25-30.
[12] H. F. Clarizio, *Toward Positive Classroom Discipline*, New York: John Wiley & Sons, 1971, p. 100.

Punishment, no matter what form it takes (spankings, slaps, removal of a toy, sending a child to his room) tells your child *one* thing—and *one* thing only—what *not* to do. When you punish your child for touching a lamp, all he learns is not to touch the lamp. He does not learn what he can do.

Imagine yourself in your living room with a lamp, a stereo set, and a grandfather clock. If you punish your child for touching the lamp, and that is *all you do*, he will only learn to stay away from the lamp. Next, he may begin playing with the stereo set. If you punish him for that behavior he will learn not to play with the stereo set, but again, that is all he will learn. Finally he'll take a shot at the clock, which will likely result in more punishment. Despite the fact that he has learned three things not to do, he has yet to learn what he *can do*. Punishment, then, is not a very effective teacher for long-term behavior, particularly when it is used by itself.

Even before punishment can teach a child what not to do, care must be taken to apply the punishment as close to the misbehavior as possible. This is particularly true when using punishment with young children who have yet to develop a very extensive vocabulary. Verbal explanations as to why a behavior is being punished will be ineffective unless the child can understand what is being said to him. From a practical standpoint, it is often difficult for a parent to punish a behavior immediately after it has occurred. The parent may not be close by or not even know that the behavior occurred for some time. If the parent still punishes, even though there has been a delay between behavior and the parent's reaction, the punishment will not be very effective. In fact, the parent may end up punishing a behavior that she did not intend to decrease.

There is also a rather ironic observation often seen when punishment is used. Reactions that *you* may consider to be punishing may not be punishing to your child. In other words, your "punishment" may end up being more like positive reinforcement. For example, you spank your child for some misbehavior. As far as you are concerned, a spanking should be a form of punishment. But let's assume that you have accidentally fallen into the habit of paying attention to your child primarily when he misbehaves. The attention that you are giving is in the form of a spanking, and your child may put up with the spanking in order to have you attend to him. In such a situation, the child may begin to work hard (misbehave) for your attention, or for your spanking! His misbehavior will increase, even though you want the opposite to happen. Now that I have mentioned these three "problems" with punishment, let us see what can be done about them.

First, punishment, no matter what form it takes, *must* be used in conjunction with positive reinforcement. This is an extremely important point that must be emphasized. By using positive reinforcement along with one of the several procedures that are employed to decrease behavior, our children stand a much better chance of learning precisely what we wish for them to do. They will not only learn which behaviors to avoid (playing with the lamp), but they will also learn which behavior you deem acceptable (playing with toys, reading books). In addition to teaching both desired and undesired behaviors, the combination of positive reinforcement and punishment almost makes it impossible for a parent to give the majority of his attention to his child's misbehavior. The parent seeks out the desired behavior and shows his child a positive means of gaining attention.

Second, it is very important that your punishing reactions come as close to the misbehavior as possible. There is an automatic effect that takes place when we use positive reinforcement or punishment to teach desired and undesired behaviors. This automatic effect is almost always observed with young children. Based on the research[13] of Drs. Jack Michael, Lee Meyerson, and others, it is now quite clear that *whatever behavior immediately precedes* the application of positive reinforcement or punishment is the behavior that is going to be affected by either of the procedures. If we *intend* to punish behavior *A*, but our punishment immediately follows behavior *B*, behavior *B* is the behavior most likely to be affected. An example of this situation can be easily seen in the "Wait until your father gets home" approach. Assume your child has misbehaved in the morning, and all you do is to tell him that he is going to be punished when his father comes home. Eight hours later, Father arrives, and you tell him that *his* son misbehaved and he will have to punish him. If Father does punish the child for the behavior that occurred much earlier in the day, the punishment will more than likely affect whatever the child was doing immediately prior to the application of the punishment instead of what he had done earlier. Even a verbal explanation with a young child may not mediate the long delay.

[13] J. Michael and L. Meyerson, "A Behavioral Approach to Counseling and Guidance." *Harvard Educational Review*, 1962, *32*, pp. 382-402.

Let me suggest some guidelines for *not* punishing when there is a delay between misbehavior and consideration of punishment.

1. If you cannot punish the undesired behavior immediately, and your child does not have the verbal skills to understand why the punishment is being given, punishment should be avoided.

2. If your child has the necessary verbal skills to understand your explanation for why punishment is coming, but his misbehavior was not of a serious type (you must determine what is serious), and he is presently behaving desirably, punishment should be avoided. In its place a verbal warning to the effect that the misbehavior should not occur again may be sufficient.

3. If the behavior was very serious, but your child lacks the verbal skills and a long delay has occurred, there is not a great deal you can do other than to try to prevent access to that behavior again. Telling your one-year-old child that he is being spanked for playing with the electric socket one minute ago will not result in a decrease in that behavior unless the child knows precisely what an electric socket is. What he is doing at the time the spanking is given is the behavior that will be affected.

In summary, keep two points in mind as we proceed through this chapter. First, to be most effective, punishment must be used in conjunction with positive reinforcement; second, punishment, like positive reinforcement, needs to be applied as close to the behavior as possible.

BEHAVIOR PAIRS: THE KEY TO TEACHING CHILDREN WHAT TO DO AS WELL AS WHAT NOT TO DO

Read the next few sentences, then close the book and note your reactions to your child's behavior for several hours. Watch for the number of times you react in a negative way to some misbehavior while also watching the number of times you react in a positive way to some behavior that is as close to being opposite to the misbehavior as possible.

What did you find? If you are like many parents you probably responded more often to something your child did that was displeasing to you than you responded to some behavior that was desirable. In a very true sense, many of us are lazy. We have fallen into the habit of not paying any attention to desirable behavior while reacting quite strongly to annoying or disruptive behaviors. I'm certain that we do not mean to do this, but our busy schedules sometimes set the stage for ignoring our children when they are being good. It is relatively easy to pay little attention to a child when he is doing just what you want him to do. When the child is good, it gives us a chance to do housework, or prepare dinner, or read a novel, or perhaps, just rest. Unfortunately, it is this lack of attention at the "quiet" or good times that gets many of us in trouble. However, thinking about behavior pairs can help us avoid this trouble.

You recall that behavior pairs are sets of behaviors that are incompatible to one another. There is crying and noncrying (or being quiet). There is playing with a lamp and playing with crayons. A child cannot be behaving desirably and misbehaving at the same time. We always try to teach our child to do one of the behaviors, while teaching him to avoid doing the other. To do this, we combine procedures. We use positive reinforcement to teach the desired half of the behavior pair, and we use one of the various procedures to decrease behavior to teach the avoidance of the undesired half of the behavior pair.

Think back for a moment to what you observed about your own behavior during the several suggested hours of noting your reactions to your child's behavior. Did you tell your child not to run in the house? What did you do when you saw him walking in the house? Did you punish him for pulling a toy away from his sister? Did you reinforce him when he was sharing his toys? If you took television privileges away from your daughter because she did not clean up her room, what did you do when she did clean up the room? Think once more how easy it can be for us to ignore desirable behavior?

PUNISHMENT: SPANKINGS, SLAPS, AND YELLING

Psychologists who write books to parents on child-rearing, by their own decision, are always reticent about discussing physical punishment. The reasons for our apprehension are quite simple. First, we would much prefer to talk to the parent directly so that there will be no misunderstanding as to what is being said. Second, we know from experience that many parents, even before reading the book, are already using entirely too much physical punishment where other approaches would be much better. Third, we know that if punishment is used excessively, parents will begin to observe any or all of the following: their children will learn not only to avoid certain behaviors (some that were not even punished), but they will also learn to avoid the people who do the punishing—their parents; their children may begin to show an increase in aggressive type behaviors—such would be the case where the parent spanks a child and the child, in turn, spanks a younger brother; and their children will begin to experience fear—and fear and understanding why punishment is coming do not go hand in hand.

Still, we know that despite the potential serious side effects of physical punishment, parents do use it, and the reality of life indicates that, at times, it is warranted. Many psychologists recognize this fact, and several of them have written their opinions.

Dr. Wesley Becker and colleagues state:[14]

"There are few mothers of two-year-olds who question the use of punishment when it keeps their children from being hurt or killed by automobiles, knives, gas, or fire."

Dr. Albert Bandura states:[15]

"Few would criticize the use of punishment in teaching young children to stay out of busy streets, to keep their hands off of hot stoves, or to refrain from inserting metal objects in electric sockets."

As a result of the clear realization that children must be taught to avoid certain behaviors, the ultimate questions regarding physical punishment are not, "physical punishment—yes or no," but the following.

1. What behaviors are you considering punishing? Is the behavior serious enough to warrant a spank or slap?
2. How forceful will the punishment be? Will you be able to punish and be reasonably calm at the same time?
3. Will you be willing to spend considerably more effort reinforcing alternative desired behaviors? Will you seek out the desired, incompatible member of the behavior pair?

[14] W. C. Becker, S. Engelmann, and D. R. Thomas, *Teaching: A Course In Applied Psychology*, Chicago: Science Research Associates, 1971, p. 155.

[15] A. Bandura, *Principles of Behavior Modification*, New York: Holt, Rinehart and Winston, 1969. (Statement in Clarizio, *Toward Positive Classroom Discipline*, p. 100.)

4. Is there another approach you can use that will bring about the desired decrease in the misbehavior?

One of the first things you will need to do is to make some decision as to which behaviors warrant physical punishment. Decide which of your child's behaviors are annoying to *you*, and which ones are dangerous to him or others who are close by. In this case, dangerous means the possibility that he or others will experience some physical harm as a result of his behavior. Running out into a street, playing with matches or electric sockets, or throwing rocks at a younger brother are examples of dangerous behaviors. Whining, crying, dropping food on the floor, wetting a bed, or bouncing a ball in the house are behaviors that are more annoying than anything else. It is very important that you spend time considering these two categories of behavior. You and your spouse will need to maintain a consistent approach in order to increase the rapidity with which the learning will take place. Also, it is absolutely critical that you keep the number of physically punishing reactions to a minimum. You will need to reserve the use of physical punishment for those behaviors that you believe must be stopped immediately.

There are many beneficial reasons for keeping physical punishment to a minimum. First, there is a greater chance that your punishment will maintain its effectiveness—your child will not get used to the punishment. In this way, you can avoid having to increase its intensity. Second, you will be able to avoid associating yourself too often with the punishment and, therefore, your child will not learn to avoid you. Third, and most important, you will be able to decrease the frequency with which future punishment will be necessary. Your child will quickly learn that for his benefit, you mean business. You are clearly telling him to avoid running into the street or to avoid investigating electric sockets. For his sake, he must learn to avoid such activities. Again, take a few extra minutes considering which of your child's behaviors must be stopped immediately. If you find yourself having some difficulty determining which behaviors are dangerous, talk with your pediatrician. Considering the use of physical punishment is too critical an issue not to take advantage of all available professional help.

If you can get to your child's behavior immediately and it is of a serious type, then a *single, calm, medium force* spank on the bottom is all that should be necessary. If your child is touching something that you can not remove and it is potentially dangerous, then a *single, calm, medium force* slap on the touching hand will be just as effective. In both cases, *precede* your spank or slap with a clearly spoken "No!" Say the word "No" even if your child is preverbal. By doing so, the verbal statement "No" will begin to acquire the properties of the spank or slap and, if you are consistent, your child will begin avoiding several behaviors as soon as the word "No" is spoken. If you will use physical punishment sparingly, a single spank should get your message across. You must be calm when you do spank, otherwise you will begin to act as a model for aggressive behaviors. Medium force, of course, is a most difficult thing to define. You want your child to learn very quickly that he has just done something you no longer want him to do. If your spanking is more like a little tap, it will not be very effective, particularly if he has several pairs of pants on. On the other hand, do not use too much force. The object of a spank is to inform your child that what he has done is not acceptable—and that is its sole object.

After talking with many parents and professionals in the field of child rearing, the general conclusion most often reached is that there is absolutely *no* need to ever use any form of physical punishment with a child who has yet to begin to crawl. Up to that point, objects of danger should be removed from his proximity. He simply should not be allowed to get himself in any kind of trouble. Even beyond the crawling stage, spanks and slaps should be extremely limited. In fact, if you think about it, there are only a few ways a child might hurt himself during the crawling stage—hanging on draperies or pulling objects off tables. If you decide to teach your child to avoid those type of things, if you are consistent, one or two slaps on the touching hand should be sufficient.

Now to the most important issue that was raised in question three. Will you be willing to spend considerably more effort reinforcing alternative desired behavior? Will you seek out the desired, incompatible member of the behavior-pair? The key to keeping physical punishment, or any type of punishment, for that matter, to an absolute minimum, is the use of positive reinforcement with an alternative desired behavior. You must teach your child what he can do. Therefore, when he plays with his toys or reads a book, make certain that you reinforce those behaviors. By doing so you are teaching him not only what to do, but you are also teaching him a means of *avoiding* further punishment.

If you have been very consistent with the few spanks or slaps needed to teach your child to avoid dangerous behaviors, and you have used positive reinforcement to teach your child alternative appropriate behaviors, you may be able to avoid using future physical punishment. The older a child becomes, the less physical punishment should be necessary. There are other methods for decreasing behavior that are much more effective in the long run than spankings. I would say that the vast majority of times parents use physical punishment with an older child is when the *parents* have lost their "cool" instead of when the child has done something dangerous.

Before moving on, let me say a quick word about yelling. Usually, the one who benefits the most from yelling is the one who *does* the yelling—not the recipient. Yelling and its accompanying annoyance to everyone is one of the most frequent complaints I hear about, not only from parents but also from their children. No one seems to like it very much, yet we still do it. At times, it is just difficult not to yell. But the frequency of yelling can and should be reduced to a minimum. What needs to be done is to make certain that the mutually agreed on rules, regulations, and consequences for house hold behaviors are clearly understood by all members of the family. When a rule is broken, the individual who has misbehaved knows that he has done so. He also knows what the consequences will be. All you need to do is to carry through with the decided consequences. This should be done in a very calm, relaxed manner—or at least as calm as you can make it. If you will be consistent with your reactions, you can very often put a stop to annoying behavior by giving *one* clearly stated warning signal that the misbehavior must end. In the event that it doesn't end, then immediately carry through with whatever your family has determined is the necessary action. In a somewhat lighter vein, I recall some research that suggests that garden weeds die if they are yelled at. If that is true, you can still express your frustration and save money on herbicides at the same time.

PUNISHMENT: THE REMOVAL OF MATERIAL POSITIVE REINFORCERS

The most effective way to deal with many behaviors that are not physically dangerous to a child is by removing or withholding a material reinforcer that is as closely related to the misbehavior as possible. An example follows. Instead of spanking a child for leaving his bicycle parked in the driveway when he has been told several times to put the bike away in the garage, you should withhold riding privileges for that day or the following day as a form of punishment. If you will do this and then socially reinforce him for putting the bike away when the privilege is reinstated, you will be using a very effective means of reacting to the behavior pair. Another example of this approach can be seen when many parents teach their children that coloring or painting can only take place in one or two locations in their home. A chair and table (along with supplies) is provided, and as long as the child remains in that location, he can enjoy all that creative coloring has to offer. However, if he begins to color on something other than what was provided, the parents say "No," and they remove the crayons for a short period of time. After the brief period of the loss of the crayons, the child is taken back in his chair and the supplies are returned.

There are many advantages for using the withdrawal of reinforcers as a method for teaching children what not to do. First, you are able to avoid being a model for aggressive behaviors. Second, according to Dr. Bandura's research,[16] removal of positive reinforcers does not generate the kind of emotional reactions—primarily fear—that are seen when physical punishment is used. Third, and very important, inherent in the removal of a material reinforcer is the possibility of earning it back. Once the child begins to behave as the parent desires, the reinforcer is returned and the child learns what to do as well as what not to do.

One of the more difficult practical aspects of removing material reinforcers is the question of how long should the reinforcer be withheld. Most parents seem to do a pretty good job of determining the length of the punishing period. As I see it, the key to the withholding of reinforcers as an effective means for teaching children what not to do rests with the idea that the reinforcers are returned *as soon as* the child begins to behave as his parents desire. As such, time is *not* the barometer you should use to determine when the reinforcer should be reinstated. Instead, it is the child's behavior that should be the deciding factor. For example, television is withheld until a child successfully completes his homework. The reinforcer of TV, in this example, is solely dependent on homework behavior. The advantage of this approach is that the child is basically in *control* of *his* reinforcer. This is very important for as Dr. Krumboltz has pointed out.[17] "The aversive condition should be easy for a child to terminate when his behavior improves."

[16] Bandura, op cit., pp. 338-348.
[17] Krumboltz, op cit., p. 187.

It has been suggested that this approach will aid a child in developing independence and "self-directedness." The idea behind the development of these characteristics is that the child will quickly see that his behavior results in reasonably predictable consequences—assuming his parents are consistent. He will see that his behavior has purpose, that it is meaningful to his parents. He will be able to say to himself, "When I do this, such and such happens, and when I do this, such and such will happen." The child learns that he has a choice. He will also learn what will probably occur as a result of his choice.

Mickey and Her Sandbox

Two-year-old Mickey loved to play in her sandbox. Her favorite game was to fill an old pot with sand and deposit the sand in various locations in her backyard. Her parents had repeatedly asked her to keep the sand in the box, but Mickey seemed to forget to do so. One morning, after several requests, Mickey was spanked when she failed to keep the sand in the sandbox. Mother also took the pot away—placing it in the kitchen. Mickey was very upset, and she cried for some time. On the following morning she was given the pot, but before long the pot and its contents found their way to a newly planted flower garden.

After realizing that the repeated warnings, the spanking, and the removal of the pot had all failed to teach Mickey to keep the pot and the sand in the sandbox, Mother tried a different approach. Mickey was placed in the sandbox with the pot and her mother pulled her chair close to where her daughter was playing. As was usually the case, Mickey played in the box for several minutes. During this time, Mother made certain she praised her daughter for keeping the pot and sand in the box. After about 10 minutes, Mickey stepped from the box with the pot in her hand. Immediately Mother removed the pot from Mickey, telling her that she could only play with her toy while she was sitting in the box. After a minute or so of crying, Mickey returned to the box and Mother immediately returned the pot. This approach was carried on for the better part of an hour, during which time Mickey left the box with the pot on two occasions. Each time Mickey left, the pot was removed. It was returned when Mickey returned.

On the following day, the same procedure was used and Mickey did very well. After a short period, Mother returned her chair to where she usually sat while still praising her daughter for the desired playing. Mickey did take the pot from the box after Mother moved, but Mother immediately removed the pot and waited until Mickey sat in the box for a few moments before returning the pot to her daughter. After that, the pot stayed almost exclusively in the sandbox.

There are a whole host of "what not to do's" and "what to do's" that can be taught by removing and returning reinforcers. In many cases, the return of the reinforcer is dependent on the child offering us some assurance that he will do as we ask. As you well know, assurances and actual behavior are not always the same. You must try to reinforce behavior instead of just an assurance. For example, a toy that is thrown in the house can be removed for a short period of time and returned when the child promises not to throw it again. If he does throw it again, even though he promises to do otherwise, it is important to again remove the toy, but for a longer period of time. How long that time period should be is difficult to determine, but it should be long enough to tell the child that he will lose access to the toy for some time when it is thrown. This same approach can be used when excessive fighting or splashing is observed in a swimming pool. As a result of the misbehavior, the child loses a certain amount of time to play in the pool. He is allowed to return only when he indicates that the misbehavior will not occur again. If he keeps his word, then all is fine. However, if it is an "empty" promise, then the child should lose pool privileges for a greater length of time.

Robert's Flying Bat

In his enthusiasm to learn to hit a ball, Robert would fling his plastic bat about 20 feet when he would strike out. His father was a student of the game, having played it for his college team. He wanted to help his son learn to hit the ball, but more important, he wanted him to learn to control his temper and no longer throw his bat when he would strike out.

Most of Robert's practice sessions took place in his backyard. His father would serve as pitcher, his mother would play both outfield and infield, and his younger sister would usually just get in the way. Each of the family would take turns hitting the ball, although Robert ended up having about three times more batting practice than the rest of his family combined.

Robert was told that the next time the bat was thrown he would have to sit on the sidelines until he was ready to practice and no longer throw his bat. He was told that it is certainly okay to be upset when striking out, but he could no longer throw his bat. Robert agreed, and everything went well for the next two times he struck out. He was warmly praised for being a good sport. However, on his following turn, the bat went flying. Father immediately placed Robert in a chair on the patio, reminding him that he would not be able to play for a little while since he threw the bat. Robert was upset, and he exclaimed that he didn't want to play anyway. He sat on the chair while his sister took her turn. After about five minutes, Robert asked his father if he could have another turn. "Only if you promise not to throw the bat," was Father's reply. The very next time Robert failed to hit the ball, the bat was thrown. As if to indicate that he knew he had done something wrong, he immediately apologized and promised not to do it again. Father, however, sent him to his chair, telling Robert that although he appreciated his apology he, nevertheless, did throw the bat and he would have to sit out for 15 minutes. Robert put up quite a fuss, but he drew little attention from his family. After the 15-minute period, Robert returned to the game. Although he still was upset when he failed to connect with the ball, the bat throwing had ceased.

AS YOU MIGHT HAVE GUESSED—REMOVAL AND RETURN OF MATERIAL REINFORCERS CAN WORK AGAINST YOU

Your behavior and mine is greatly affected by the results of our reactions to our children. This means that when we do something that results in a desired outcome from our children, *we* are being reinforced and *we* will probably repeat our reaction in the future. Suppose, for example, that our child has thrown one of his toys while playing by himself. I have suggested that one of the ways this can be dealt with is by removing the toy instead of spanking the child. Suppose further that you decide to try my suggestion. There is a very good chance that your child will not like having his toy removed. He may begin to cry or whine over the fact that he has been punished. If the whining becomes very annoying, you will be placed under a certain amount of pressure to put a stop to the whining. You may find—quite accidentally—that by giving the child back his toy the whining does, in fact, stop. What has happened is that your behavior of giving back the toy has been reinforced because it has resulted in an end to the annoying whining behavior. Unfortunately, your behavior has also reinforced the child's whining. Now, two behaviors will likely increase—the whining and the returning of the toy. I think you can see that the behaviors will work against one another, for each time the child whines, you will give him back his toy which, in turn, will increase his whining.

It is very important to keep in mind that whatever behavior is followed by a reinforcer will tend to increase. When you use the return of a reinforcer, watch carefully what behavior is occurring prior to the return. In the above example, instead of returning the toy while the child whines, wait for a few moments of quiet behavior and then return the toy. In this way, nonwhining, quiet behavior will most likely increase.

IGNORING BEHAVIOR: THE WITHHOLDING OF ATTENTION AND RECOGNITION

After having observed many parents react to their children's behavior, I am more convinced now then ever that one of the reasons why many of us are not very effective in teaching our children what not to do is because we work too hard at it. We react too often to behaviors that should not be reacted to at all. We sometimes make such a big fuss over a small misbehavior that before very long the minor activity becomes a major momentary problem. Even the most conscientious parent falls victim to his own frustration and reacts in a way opposite to what he would prefer. I watched a friend of mine become so upset over her daughter's minor tantrum and protestation that she spanked her child quite harshly. Everything happened so fast that I honestly believe that she was unaware of what she was doing. She felt so bad afterward that she remained upset for some time. As might be expected, all the spanking did was to intensify her child's tantrum.

Certain behaviors, of course, cannot be ignored. Behaviors that are dangerous or might lead to someone being hurt should be reacted to. But many behaviors are more annoying than anything else, and, in many cases, if no one will react to them, they will decrease.

Kathy's Plate of Food

For Christmas, Kathy received her own set of dishes. The set consisted of three plastic plates, three cups, and three small soup bowls. Each of the plates, cups, and bowls had colorful paintings of clowns, animals, and flowers, and Kathy really liked them. For whatever reason, Kathy began to insist that her meat be placed on the left side of the clown or elephant; that her potatoes be placed on the right side of the plate; and that her vegetables cover the feet of whoever was on the plate. Mother initially felt this was a game and had no objections. After a week or so, the game became annoying to both Mother and Father. One evening, Kathy became quite upset when her father refused to put the food exactly where Kathy wanted it. After a few moments of crying she was sent from the table. Both Mom and Dad felt bad about their overreaction. They discussed the situation and concluded that they were behaving foolishly. Kathy was brought back to the table, and a plate of warm food was placed before her. The big smile on her face indicated that all the food was in its proper place. The parents never said anything else about the game, and within about two weeks the location of the food seemed to make little difference to Kathy.

World War II in 1970

In the winter of 1970, Eileen's junior high school girl friends began to show great interest in wearing their father's old clothes to school. The school apparently had no objection, but Eileen's parents did. Each day the girls would vie with each other as to who was wearing the oldest, most "significant," and "meaningful" paternal garments. As a result of her parents' refusal to allow her to participate in the fad, Eileen was forced to lose out on some pleasant peer reinforcement. She began to ask her parents for some logical explanation for their refusal, but none was offered. Eileen was upset and began to demonstrate her feelings in ways that resulted in some additional disagreement between her mother and herself.

At the time of this situation, Eileen's aunt was living in the house. She did not agree with her sister's handling of the problem. She pointed out that when they were in school, they, too, had fleeting fads that ended as quickly as they began. She urged her sister and brother-in-law to allow Eileen to participate in what was going on. After much convincing from the aunt, Eileen's parents acquiesced.

That evening at dinner, Eileen's mother told her daughter that perhaps she was being too old-fashioned, and it was agreed that Eileen could wear whatever she desired. Eileen was thrilled. An intense family discussion took place as to what would be the most significant and meaningful thing to wear. Everyone seemed to enjoy the involvement. After a few moments, Father excused himself from the table saying that he had an idea. He returned shortly with a box that had been sitting in a trunk in the basement. He presented the box to his wide-eyed daughter. She quickly opened it up and, to her extreme delight, she found a well-preserved Eisenhower jacket.

To say that she was a hit at school the following day would be an understatement. If a first prize had been given, it would have been Eileen's. She wore the jacket every day for the next two weeks. But as Eileen's aunt had predicted, the jacket began to find its way back into the box and eventually into the trunk.

There are some important commonalities in these two cases. First, both sets of parents probably overreacted to their children's desires. Neither request appeared to be outlandish. I believe both parents would agree about these last two statements, particularly after their children's behaviors had run their course. Second, both parents were flexible enough to see that they probably had made an issue out of something very small. Third, and most important, both parents, as a result of their own reevaluation, associated themselves with a reinforcer strongly desired by their children. This type of an association cannot help but strengthen the relationship of the family.

Annoyance and frustration are not the only reasons why many parents react to behaviors when they probably should not. Concern that a particular behavior may be "symbolic" of a problem can also be responsible for the same situation. In some cases, the parents' concern is a result of some of psychology's own pet ghosts.

David's Natural Rhythm

I must admit that I was taken aback by David's mother's phone call when she told me that she thought her six-month-old was masturbating almost every day. She proceeded to explain that for the last week, right after David would wake up from a nap, he would begin to rock back and forth in a crawling position. The behavior apparently only occurred in his crib. She told me that she was certain this behavior was called infantile masturbation and she was becoming alarmed by it.

I indicated to her that there are some psychologists who might agree with her analysis, but that the rocking might mean many other things—none of which are cause for concern. I suggested that she call very little attention to the behavior and that she record the exact time and duration of the rocking. This was a relatively simple task, for the child's motion caused the crib to rub against the wall of his room and Mother would not have to be in the room to hear when it was happening. On occasion, she would look in on her son to see if any other movements were responsible for the rhythmic sounds.

I cannot be certain as to what happened, but by the end of the week David's mother called me to tell me that her son was no longer "doing whatever he was doing." I called her back in about a month and she told me she hadn't been aware of anymore rocking. She added that she was happy she hadn't paid much attention to it.

Up to this point I have not touched on the behavior that usually receives a great percentage of our attention. It is the behavior of crying—specifically attention-getting crying. I am mentioning it now because without question, the most effective way to reduce the occurrences of excessive attention-getting crying is to avoid reacting to it.

If the number of synonyms are any indication of the frequency with which this behavior is observed, then it must be a very frequent behavior—Scrabble players and crossword puzzle addicts take heed— wail, keen, moan, sob, bawl, flubber, whimper, yowl, clamor, exclaim, scream, shout, bellow, roar, weep.[18]

Seriously, we all know that crying is an important behavior. It is particularly important for the child who has yet to learn to communicate his discomforts verbally. Parents use crying to help them determine when their child needs attention. Prior to words such as "ouch," "hurt," and "feel bad," and nonverbal behavior such as pointing to the stomach, touching the forehead, or pointing to a new tooth, parents have had to rely almost exclusively on crying behavior for an indication of physical and emotional discomfort. (I once heard a pediatrician on the radio say that a crying child is a growing child. I'm not certain what he meant but, if we can take him literally, it means that many of us are going to have some super basketball players in our families.)

But crying occurs for reasons other than physical and emotional discomfort. Many children cry because they receive a good deal of attention for doing so. Many children cry at times because of the

[18] L. Urdang, ed., *The Random House Dictionary of the English Language*, New York: Random House, 1968, p. 322.

reactions of their parents to the crying. It is this attention-getting crying that makes our role as parents more difficult.

It is very important that you and I be able to interpret what our crying child is trying to tell us. We must be able to listen to and understand different types of crying. Many parents are very good at this. They know that certain cries are indicators of discomfort, and they know that certain cries are primarily attention getters. Usually, the children of these parents do not cry a great deal. In fact, most of the crying of their children occurs under conditions of some sort of physical discomfort. As soon as the parents hear the crying, they are reasonably assured that something is wrong, and they attend to their child's discomfort immediately. How do parents get themselves into this favorable position? How is it that some parents have developed the situation where one, they are able to interpret their child's cries, and two, they have been able to reduce the frequency of excessive attention-getting crying?

We have learned that when a behavior is followed by reinforcement, that behavior is more likely to occur in the future. What you may have guessed is that when a behavior is no longer followed by reinforcement, the behavior weakens or tends to decrease. Crying is a behavior that usually receives reinforcement very early in a child's life. This is, of course, by necessity. When the infant cries, we attend to him without any concern or consideration that we are reinforcing the crying. Even when our child is well beyond the infant stage, we still respond to his crying almost immediately. Our reactions teach our child that we will come to him when he cries. However, somewhere around three to six months of age, many parents begin to avoid attending to all their child's crying. As soon as the parent begins to select which type of crying she will attend to, she begins to teach her child to cry under certain conditions and not to cry under other conditions. For example, crying would be attended to when there was any indication of physical discomfort, but it would not be attended to when the parent was reasonably sure the child was not hurt or feeling bad.

Molly's Parents' Decision

Bill and Sue had been trying to have a child for six years. Finally, after eight years of marriage, Sue received the blessed news that she was pregnant. Molly made her appearance somewhat earlier than was predicted. Although she was in good health, she weighed just over five pounds.

Everything was fine until Molly was about seven months old. She became quite ill and started to lose weight. Although their physician assured them that Molly's illness was not critical, Bill and Sue were very concerned. For almost a month, they spent nearly 24 hours a day watching and taking care of their daughter. Molly was only out of her parents' arms for occasional periods of sleep. Her sleep, as little as there was, was restless and, as soon as she would cry or whimper, Sue or Bill would immediately pick her up and soothe her. Finally the illness subsided, and the pediatrician pronounced Molly to be in perfect health. To celebrate, as well as to relax, Bill and Sue decided to go out for dinner for the first time since Molly's illness. Bill's sister was going to baby-sit. Sue felt that her sister-in-law would be perfect, since she had spent almost as much time with Molly as Bill and Sue had.

As Bill and Sue prepared to leave the house, Molly began to cry. Sue picked Molly up and told her that they would be back very soon. The crying, however, did not stop. Instead, it increased. Sue decided to take Molly's temperature and found it to be normal. During this time, Molly's crying stopped. Reluctantly, the parents, once again, started to leave. Their departure ended when Molly began to cry. Sue put a call in to the pediatrician, and it was immediately returned. After telling the doctor of what had happened, he suggested that the parents just leave the house once having said good-bye to Molly, and if they wanted, bring Molly into his office in the morning. Sue and Bill agreed to take their physician's advice. They kissed Molly good-bye and walked out the front door. Molly began to scream loudly. Bill and Sue sat in their car for a few moments listening to their daughter. Without having to say a word to each other, they simultaneously walked back into the house and ate dinner at home.

"You've got to give yourself some free time," the physician told Sue the following morning. "I have checked Molly over, and she is fine. Don't worry, go out with Bill and relax. Believe me, that is the best thing you can do for Molly."

Dinner out or an early movie was just not to be. Each time Bill and Sue would try to leave, they would always come back because of Molly's protests. One evening, after Molly was asleep, they agreed that something had to be done. They began to look very carefully at Molly's crying and how they reacted to it. They jotted on a piece of paper the times Molly would cry most often. They found that Molly would begin to cry when she was hungry or tired. She would cry when her mother would walk away from her. She would cry most intensely when Bill and Sue would leave the house. After conversing with their pediatrician, Bill and Sue decided to try to teach Molly not to cry when Mother walked away and not to cry when Mom and Dad left the house. The following morning would be the start of their efforts.

Bill and Sue were both apprehensive in the morning. From what the pediatrician had told them, they knew that Molly was going to cry a great deal at first ("She has gotten into the habit of crying and she is not going to quit simply because you are changing the way you're reacting.") But he also told them that if they would stick with their efforts, Molly's crying would decrease, perhaps quite rapidly; that made the parents feel a little better.

As was usually the case, Molly woke up happy and smiling. Breakfast time went well. Bill kissed Molly and Sue good-bye—everything, so far, was fine. When Molly finished breakfast, Sue picked her up and they both went into the family room. Molly was placed on the floor with some toys, and Sue sat close by. In a very animated voice, Sue talked with Molly about the game she was playing. After several minutes, Sue stood up while still talking. Molly, quickly looked up, but did not cry. Sue, then, sat back down. A few more minutes passed, and Sue stood up and walked a few feet away from Molly, again still talking with her. Since there was no crying, Sue returned. This approach was used for several more minutes. Finally, Sue decided to walk from the family room into the kitchen. This would be the first test, for Molly would not be able to see her mother from the family room. The crying did not start until Mother had reached the kitchen. Instead of crawling to her mother, Molly sat on the floor and cried. Sue's first impulse was to return to the family room, but she didn't. Instead, she let Molly cry. The child cried for about 15 minutes, then she stopped. Sue waited for a few seconds of noncrying and then went back into the family room and sat next to her daughter. They played together for several minutes, and then Sue went back into the kitchen. Again, Molly started to cry—this time for about 25 minutes (the pediatrician had told Sue that the crying would increase before it would begin to decrease—and he was right). It was all Sue could do to prevent herself from going to her daughter. But the crying did stop, and Sue went back.

Sue kept this approach up for several days. She began to notice a gradual decrease in Molly's crying. She made certain that she avoided attending to Molly when she cried—when she knew nothing was wrong—while trying to be as reinforcing as possible when Molly did not cry. The procedure was working. After about five days, Molly would cry for only a few seconds when her mother walked from the room.

With a degree of success under their belts, Bill and Sue decided to try a similar approach to the problem of reducing the crying when they left the house together. Bill's sister would again be the baby-sitter. Bill's sister came over to the house about an hour before the parents were going to leave. She had prepared several games for Molly. Bill and Sue kissed Molly good-bye and walked out the house. The crying began somewhat before the front door had closed, but the parents went to their car and left. Their plan was to leave the house for only 5 or 10 minutes and then return. They, however, would wait outside until Molly was no longer crying. As it turned out, they had to sit in their car for almost 20 minutes, for apparently Molly cried from the moment they left and kept crying for about a half an hour. During that time Bill's sister tried to involve Molly into a game, but had little success. When Molly stopped crying, her parents walked into the house.

On the following day, the procedure was repeated. Again the parents went away for a short period of time and returned only when Molly stopped her crying. Gradually, they extended the time away. The crying began to decrease rapidly. Molly started to play more games with the baby-sitter. She still cried when her parents left, but for only a brief period of time.

There was a large decrease in the amount of crying described by the parents as attention-getting crying. For the first time since Molly's illness, the parents were able to go out at night. Molly still cried, but it was much easier for the parents to interpret what her crying meant.

The key to Bill and Sue's success was the combination of their consistent withholding of attention for Molly's attention-getting crying and the equally consistent reinforcement of her noncrying. Their intent, of course, was not to eliminate crying, but simply to reduce its occurrence to a point where they would be more likely to respond to Molly when she really needed them. They felt much better about the fact that they would be able to leave their daughter for a few hours with the knowledge that she would not be so upset.

One of the things that helped Molly's parents prepare for their teaching approach was their discussion regarding which behaviors they would attend to and which behaviors they would try not to attend to. This preplanning did not take a great deal of time, and it improved their chances of being very consistent with Molly's behavior. The reason why this consistency is so important is that you will need to limit to a bare minimum the number of accidental reinforcers given to attention-getting crying. Occasional attention given to this behavior will actually serve to *increase* instead of decrease it. You must also try to withhold your attention for the total duration of the crying. Once it has completely stopped for a few moments, then you should call attention to the alternative, noncrying behavior.

A Programmer's Program

Ann's mother and father were divorced when she was three months old. At the time of the divorce, Ann's mother was an electronic programmer for a large firm. I first met her in a graduate seminar I was offering at the university. The course was primarily a discussion of various ways to deal with children's behavior. One of the assignments for each member of the class was to develop a teaching program that could be used to teach a child a particular behavior. One of the students developed a program to teach her young son to ride a bicycle. Another chose to teach her 10-year-old to play the guitar. Ann's mother decided to develop a program to decrease attention-getting crying that would be used with her daughter. Prior to the development of their programs, each student had to present to the entire class some statement that would describe why they had chosen their program and what benefit the program would offer both the child and the parents. Ann's mother's presentation created more discussion than any other. There was strong disagreement among the class as to whether it was beneficial to begin teaching a six-month-old to cry less often. One student implied that the program would only be beneficial to the parent, that it would serve no purpose for the child. Another said ignoring a six-month-old could result in serious emotional damage. And a third said that the amount of cooing and babbling would also be affected.

Ann's mother asked for some time to consider the arguments. Because of the interest expressed by all the members of the class, she was given as much time as she desired. After a couple of days, Ann's mother gave her presentation.

"I have broken my presentation down into three sections," she began. "First, I want to talk about the benefits for this program for both Ann and myself. Second, I want to mention something about ignoring a child, and third, I want to tell you what I am going to do about Ann's talking."

"I believe that it is very important for children and parents to have a good, warm relationship. Much more than just loving each other, also liking each other—wanting to spend time with each other. I believe when parents and children act as the other desires—not necessarily all of the time, but at least some of the time—it is easier to like each other. I think it is easier to show love and affection to a child when he does something you like. This doesn't mean that you do not love him when he misbehaves, but it is more difficult to show love and affection when there is a lot of misbehavior."

"For me, crying is very annoying—not all crying, just a lot of it. It may not bother you, but in all honesty, it bothers me. I become annoyed and short-tempered when Ann cries a lot. When I feel this way I am not as patient with her as I would like to be. I don't punish her, but I am just not as nice to her. I do not like myself when I lose my temper, but I still do it sometimes. I know that if I can teach her to cry less often it will be better for both of us. I won't lose my temper as much, and I will be more patient and loving. I cannot see how this will not be of great benefit to Ann."

"And I am not going to ignore her. In fact, I am going to pay a lot of attention to her. But I am going to pay more attention to her when she is not crying. I am still going to comfort her when I know she is not feeling well, but I am not going to pay as much attention to her when I know she is not feeling bad or not hurt. You know what I mean, like when she drops a toy on her foot and she starts to cry. I'll look to see if her foot is okay, but I am not going to make a big deal out of it. When she stops her crying, I'll play with her. Do you see what I mean? The more she does not cry, the more I'll feel like having fun with her. She will end up getting more love and affection from me then she is now."

"As far as her talking is concerned, I just don't know. She talks an awful lot now—not really talking, but funny sounds. I love to say back to her the sounds she says to me. I am not going to stop doing this, so I don't see why she should stop. In fact, she might even do it more, since she will be crying less—I hope."

The program was relatively simple. Ann's mother had come up with several questions that she would ask herself as soon as she heard Ann cry. The questions referred to the following areas: Feeding schedule—

how long had it been since Ann had eaten? If she had recently eaten, did she have a gas bubble? Tired—how long had it been since Ann had a nap? Wet diaper—did Ann need changing? Could her diaper be to tight? Boredom—did Ann have something interesting to play with? Has Ann been given any attention for playing nicely? And pain—had Ann hurt herself?

As soon as Ann began to cry, Mother would very quickly run down her memorized check list. As soon as she discovered what was responsible for the crying, she would attend to the difficulty. When Ann's mother believed everything was fine, the crying would go unattended. As soon as the crying stopped for a few moments, Ann would receive much praise and affection. Ann was going to be as consistent as she could. She would keep some records of how long and how often Ann cried. She would also keep a record of how she was reacting to the crying so she could look at her own behavior.

After the fourth week of the teaching program, Ann's mother reported on her daughter's progress. Although Ann still cried, the crying was much less than when the program first started. The child's cooing had not changed much. What had changed was the number of times Ann's mother had lost her temper. She said she was more calm and relaxed and she was sure that Ann could "see" the change.

Ann's mother kept records of her own behavior so she could see what she was doing. Sometimes just being made aware of the number of times we are unknowingly reacting to a behavior is enough to help us change our own reactions.

Joey, How Many Times Have I Told You?

Dinner time at Joey's house was like a dull professor's lecture—much was said, but little was accomplished. Joey would put up such a fuss about eating that no one enjoyed the dinner hour. "Do you know how many times you tell him to eat his dinner?" Father asked Joey's mother. "Maybe once or twice—he has to eat," she answered. "First of all, you tell him at least 10 times each time we sit down to eat. Second, even if you think it is only twice, he still isn't eating," Father responded. "You're exaggerating, as you always do," was Mother's reply.

Realizing the conversation was getting nowhere, Joey's father decided to try something. Without telling his wife, he brought a small golf stroke counter, which was worn on his wrist, to the dinner table. Each time Mother made some comment to the effect that Joey should eat his dinner, Father pushed the pin, which registered the push on the counter. That night at dinner, Father recorded five "eat your dinner statements." After dinner was over, he showed his wife the counter. He explained that the number five in the small box represented the number of times she had told her son to eat, which he still did not do. "You're kidding," was Mom's surprised reaction.

On the following night, Father did not wear the counter. Instead, he placed it by the side of his plate. For the first 15 minutes of dinner, Mother said nothing. Joey did not eat very much, but at least there weren't any reminders. Finally, Mother could no longer contain herself. "Joey how many times do I have to tell you to eat your dinner?" Click! Realizing that her husband was keeping count, Mother laughed, as did Father. Before dinner was over, Mother gave forth with one more complete "eat your dinner" and one "eat, . . ." before she caught herself. "I am not going to say it once tomorrow night," Mother said jokingly.

On the following night, Father gave the counter to his wife and asked her to keep track of her "eat" statements. She agreed to do so, indicating that she wouldn't need it because she wasn't going to remind Joey anymore. If he didn't eat, that would be his choice.

Whether due to luck or effort, Mother did not tell her son to eat even once. In fact, over the next three dinner meals, Joey was left on his own to decide whether he should eat. Once Mom and Dad had finished their meals and had spent a few moments talking about the day's activities, the dinner plates were removed. After a few more days of not reminding Joey, he began to eat most of his food. One night he turned to his mother, while at the table, and asked her, "How come you aren't telling me to eat anymore?" After picking up the fork that had dropped out of her hand, she turned to Joey and said, "Why do you ask?"

"I don't know, I . . . ah . . . I don't know."

PUNISHMENT: THE WITHHOLDING OF ALL REINFORCEMENT UNTIL A DESIRED BEHAVIOR OCCURS

The combined withholding of material and social reinforcement for a period of time is referred to as "time-out" from reinforcement. It is a procedure that can be and, in many cases, should be used in place of physical punishment. This method has been successfully used with behaviors such as hitting, throwing sharp objects, and severe tantrums. If it is used correctly it can teach a child to avoid these types of behaviors in a surprisingly short period of time.

To show you how the procedure should be used, let me present a case study that was written by Jane Zeilberger and her colleagues.[19] The child was a four-and-a-half-year-old boy. At the time of the research, the child's mother had complained that her son was very physically aggressive. He would hit, push, kick, and throw objects. He would frequently yell and scream; he would boss other children and adults around; and he would rarely follow his parents' request. To alter these behaviors, the following instructions were given to the child's parents.

Modification of a Child's Problem Behavior with the Mother as Therapist

1. Immediately after R. acts aggressively or disobediently, take him to the time-out (TO) room. One of the family bedrooms was modified for this use by having toys and other items of interest to the child removed.
2. As R. is taken to the TO room for aggressive behavior, say "you cannot stay here (location the child was being aggressive) if you fight." As R. is taken to the TO room for disobedient behavior, say "you cannot stay here if you do not do what you are told." Make *no* other comments.
3. Place R. in the TO room swiftly and without conversation other than the above. Place him inside and shut and hook the door.
4. Leave R. in the TO room for 2 minutes. If he tantrums or cries, time the 2 minutes from the end of the last tantrum or cry.
5. When the time is up take R. out of the TO room and back to his regular activities without further comment on the episode—in a matter-of-fact manner.
6. Do not give R. explanations of the program, of what you do, of his behavior, or engage in discussions of these topics with him. If you desire to do this, have such discussions at times when the undesired behaviors have not occurred, such as later in the evening. Keep these brief and at a minimum.

[19] Jane Zeilberger, S. E. Sampen, and H. N. Sloane, "Modification of a Child's Problem Behaviors in the Home with the Mother as a Therapist." *Journal of Applied Behavior Analysis*, 1968, *1*, p. 49.

7. Ignore undesirable behavior which does not merit going to the TO room. "Ignore" means you should not comment upon such behavior, nor attend to it by suddenly looking around when it occurs.

8. Ignore aggressive or disobedient behavior which you find out about in retrospect. If you are present, treat disobedient behavior to other adults the same as disobedient behavior to you.

9. Reinforce desirable cooperative play frequently (at least once every five minutes) without interrupting it . . . .

10. Always reward R. when he obeys.

11. Special treats, such as cold drinks, cookies, or new toys or activities, should be brought out after periods of desirable play.

12. Follow the program 24 hours a day.

The outcome of the procedure was very effective, and the consistency of the parents brought about rapid and lasting change in their child's behavior. The child quickly learned that it was much more fun to behave as his parents desired and thereby avoid having to go to the time-out room.

Many parents have used such a procedure, but their efforts are not always successful. There are several reasons for this, and it is important for us to know what the reasons are. Time-out is a procedure that we do not like to use unless it is absolutely necessary. When we do use it, we want it to work quickly so that we don't have to use it often.

The first reason for our lack of success is that the misbehaving child is often sent to his room where he has access to toys, radios, stereos, TVs, and many other fun things. As such, the child is *not* being sent *from* reinforcement but *to* reinforcement. (Did you ever have a teacher who sent you from her classroom as a form of punishment and made you sit in the hallway with three or four of your friends? That's not a very effective system to decrease misbehavior.) Second, because none of us wish to appear mean to our child, we often talk to him a great deal prior to sending him to his room. Our conversation is usually very reinforcing. Note that when we talk to him immediately after he misbehaves, we are actually attending to the misbehavior. Accidentally, we may be maintaining the very behavior the child is being punished for, and that's not fair to our child. Third, and very important, is the amount of time the child must stay in his room. Time is *not* the critical factor; that is why Zeilberger told the parents to remove the child from the time-out room when he was *quiet* for two minutes. It is the quiet behavior that is the key issue. If we remove the child while he is screaming, we will be reinforcing the tantrum. On the other hand, if the child is forced to stay in his room for some fixed period of time, say 30 minutes, then he may be behaving appropriately for many minutes and not be reinforced for it. Fourth, we sometimes forget to reinforce appropriate alternative behavior. The Zeilberger parents were urged to strongly reinforce any and all desired behavior. Remember, all the procedures we use to teach the child what not to do, do only that. You must, therefore, watch your own behavior. If you do not show your child an appropriate means of gaining your attention, he will not know what you want him to do—and time-out will not tell him.

Whenever a time-out approach is used, keep the following four points in mind:

1. *The child must know what he is being punished for.* If your child can understand your explanation, give him *one* brief explanation so he will know what it was that was wrong. This explanation can serve as a warning signal prior to the use of time-out. If he has been warned once, do not offer him another explanation until he is behaving appropriately. If your child is too young to understand your verbal explanation, you will need to be very consistent and place him in the time-out room immediately upon observing the misbehavior. He will understand your message.
2. *The child must know what he has to do in order to end the punishing situation.* If your child can understand your explanation, give him *one* brief statement of what he has to do. "When you are quiet for a few minutes and are ready to play nicely, you may come out of the room." Since you will probably say this to him on the way to the room, or inside the room, make certain that you only tell him once. Otherwise you will be attending too much to the misbehavior. If your child cannot understand what you are saying, then simply remove him from the room as soon as he is quiet for two minutes. If you will be consistent he will learn that the punishing situation will end as soon as he is quiet for a few moments.
3. *When the appropriate behavior has been observed in the time-out room for two minutes or so, the punishing situation must end.* It is critical that you teach your child that *he* controls the ending of the

punishing conditions. As Dr. Krumboltz has said,[20] "The child remains in control of his behavior. He is free to terminate the aversive situation whenever he chooses to behave properly. He is not powerless as he is when punishment continues regardless of his behavior."

4. *Once the child is out of the time-out room and is behaving properly, reinforce a behavior that is incompatible to the one that he was sent to the room for.* Your child may have found out accidentally that the easiest way to obtain your attention, even though negative, is to misbehave. If that is true, the time-out procedure will not be very effective. He may be willing to take the brief time-out period in order for you to continue to attend to his misbehavior. To avoid such a problem, watch *your* behavior. Make certain that you attend to something he is doing that you approve of.

SUMMARY

I am certain you know that the procedures that we have looked at are neither brand new nor are they cure-alls. They are, however, tried and, in many cases, proven approaches. What is most interesting to me is my observation that almost every parent I know has at one time or another used each of the techniques. Although they have developed their own unique variations of the procedures, successful parents appear to have several things in common. First, they are quite consistent. They plan together what they are going to do. When possible, they involve their children in the planning. It becomes a family effort, and consistency comes a little easier. Second, they have their problems, and they do use punishment. But punishment is minimal, and yelling is equally rare. Third, they do try to catch their children being good. Not necessarily only "big" things, but many, many small good things. One cannot help but see a great number of "thank you's," smiles, and words of praise and recognition. Their homes become fun places in which to live.

Much of what we have talked about strikes of "common sense." Perhaps to you it does. But sometimes when you and I get all wrapped up in a problem, our common sense takes a vacation. We find ourselves doing things we promised we would never do. If you think you are in that kind of situation, take an emotional break. When the house is

[20] Krumboltz, op cit., p. 184.

quiet, sit back with whatever you sit back with and take a good look at what you see. Take a piece of paper and a pencil and write down what is happening. See if you can find a minor difficulty to work with. Once you experience a little bit of success in changing your behavior as well as your child's, your confidence will grow dramatically. Those 4:30 dinner hour blues and those prebedtime hassles won't just go away in a day, but with some effort they will improve.

Consistency– Plain, but Not so Simple

"Do me one favor, Doc, don't tell us that we have to be consistent. We know it, you know it, the whole world knows it, but we are the ones who have to do it. Let me put it to you this way—I experience about 12 different moods a day, that's on a good day. My wife experiences about twice that many every 15 minutes. Now, with a little incorrect math, I figure that when we are together, we might feel any one of 1,000 different ways. My guess is that our Beth is the only child in the world who has never been reacted to in the same way twice. Listen, if this consistency stuff is so important, why don't you move in with us? Then you can be the, . . . umm, . . . what do you say . . . engineer?

Suppose a mother decides it is time for her young son to "learn" a simple arithmetic problem. She has decided to teach Johnny to add two and two. In order to make my point, let us assume that Mother believes the answer to be four, while Father insists the answer is five.

Father is at work, and Mother sits her little one down and begins to teach him to say four when she asks him how much two and two are. The first time the question is presented, the child hesitates briefly. Because he is four years old and has four sisters, he responds, "Four!"

"That's right," Mother says. "You are such a smart young man, two and two are four. Let's try once more. How much are two and two?"

Johnny, somewhat overwhelmed by all the attention he received after saying "four," happily repeats the same response and is again showered with many loving words, soft caresses, and a chocolate chip cookie. Johnny is now anxiously awaiting his dad's homecoming. After all, Mother was so pleased—"I wonder what my father will do?"

Enter Father, tired from a hard day, happy to see his son, and curious as to why he is so excited. "Hey, Dad," Johnny says. "Listen to this. I know how much two and two are—they're four!"

"WHO told you that?" Father asks in a stern voice.

The son, now dismayed at the lack of enthusiasm and taken aback by the tone of his father's voice, quietly indicates that his mother taught him. "She even hugged me and gave me a cookie."

"Well, I am sorry," says Father. "Two and two aren't four, they are five. Your mother should have known that. I am quite surprised at her." Exit Father.

Although my example is stretched, I believe it makes its point. Johnny has received two distinctly different reactions to his behavior. On the one hand, Mother has praised him and confirmed his answer of four. Father has done just the opposite. Mother has said that, in the future, when someone asks you how much two and two are, your answer four, is appropriate and it may be followed by something pleasant. Father, again, has done just the opposite.

If confusion can be defined as not knowing how to respond to a situation that has many similar properties, or appears to look very much the same to a child, then we can probably say that Johnny is confused. He might say to us, "Which response is right? What do my parents want me to do?" If Johnny continues to experience these different reactions from his parents, the probable outcome will be that he will learn to say four in the presence of his mother, while when Father is around, the answer of five will be more likely.

From a scholastic point of view the problem will be solved. Johnny will observe that more people say four. But what if Father persists? What does the child do if both parents ask him the question at the same time? We might see Johnny developing a sudden attack of stomach pains and quickly retreat to his bedroom—to avoid getting in the middle. He may learn to say nothing, or to cry, or any behavior that will enable him to avoid the potentially unpleasant situation. More than anything else, he will probably look very carefully to see who is in the room before he answers.

Suppose the same child cries a great deal, especially when he falls while playing. Even when we are certain that Johnny has not hurt himself, we still see extensive crying. If you and I were to watch one of these situations, we might see Johnny's mother going over to her son, gently picking him up, and saying to him, "Mommy is here, everything will be all right." Mother tells us that she is comforting her son and that he will stop crying. We, in fact, see that Johnny stops his crying once in Mother's arms, but we also see that he cries many times during the day—not only when falling.

Dad disagrees with the way his wife reacts to Johnny's crying. He tells us that she is too "soft" with him, that she is going to "spoil" Johnny, and that he will learn to cry when the slightest thing goes wrong. You and I see that Father does not react to his son's crying unless he really hurts himself. When Johnny continues to cry, Dad loses his patience. Sometimes he spanks Johnny, which usually results in more crying. When this happens, Mom becomes very upset. She goes over to her son and comforts him. This irritates Father. While Mother is *holding* and *comforting* her son, Father *yells* something at him.

Again, Johnny has received two distinctly different reactions to his behavior. In one instance, his mother has told him it is acceptable to cry when falling (as well as other times.) She has shown that she will do various things—comfort and hold him—when he cries. Johnny has learned what his mother will do.

Father has done just the opposite. He has told his son that he will not comfort him when he cries. Furthermore, Dad has told his son that if the crying persists, he may be spanked and or yelled at. Johnny has learned what his father will do.

As with the simple arithmetic problem, Johnny will have a difficult time knowing what to do. Should he or should he not cry? Again, he will probably choose what to do only after he carefully observes who is in the room. He will have an equally difficult time behaving in a way that will be satisfactory to both his parents.

Perhaps exaggerated, what I have described is not terribly uncommon. Most people who marry come from very different backgrounds. Their ideas about children's behaviors are rarely identical. Differences in regard to how they will react to various behaviors are expected. Even more obvious than background differences are their present-day differences. It is rare that parents have the same job. Just the fact that one parent is usually home all day with the child while the other parent is away for that time is a huge difference. Father, for example, might have more patience with a whining child if he hasn't had to listen to the whining for several hours. Or Mother may be prepared for a little difficulty around dinner time because of something she has seen during the day that Father is not aware of. These, and many other factors, are surely responsible for much of the inconsistency seen between parents. Although there are no easy solutions, there are a few things you can do to make yourselves more consistent. These "things" are preplanning and communication.

Since we do differ—in our feelings, thoughts and reactions—it can be of tremendous help if we will share our differences prior to the birth of our children. That, of course, is the ideal. In the event, however, that we now find ourselves with several little ones and we have yet to honestly and clearly voice our feelings and opinions to our spouse, then this is where we must start. All I am suggesting is that we sit down and decide what we will do given a particular behavior that occurs under a particular situation. If we agree, then there is little problem. If we fail to agree, then we must compromise. The time needed for this communication is minimal, and we can make things much easier for our children and ourselves by investing the time.

There is another type of inconsistency that we should look at. This inconsistency occurs when the same parent reacts quite differently to the same or very similar behavior. One minute we might punish a particular behavior and 15 minutes later we might ignore it or reinforce it. This has to be pretty confusing to our child. Offering an idea as to why this occurs is much easier than offering a solution. A situation pops up that makes us feel on top of the world—or underneath it. Our disposition or mood changes as a result of the situation. Then our child does something, and it is only a guess as to how we will react.

Whether one has learned to bite his lip, or count to 10, or run outside and kick a weed, the idea is pretty much the same—getting a hold of oneself. Sometimes it works, and sometimes it doesn't. Something less than sage advice would be to try to keep this type of inconsistency to a minimum. You and I usually know why we are biting our lip, but our child rarely has this information. He just bares the brunt of our reactions. We are the ones who experienced the situation that just set us off; our child may not even know that the situation occurred.

Once having reacted in a way much different than usual, many parents apologize to their child and make an effort to explain what the situation was that set them off in the first place. This is a pretty honest approach. It tells our child that we are sorry for what happened and, equally as important, it tells our child that we are human.

Some parents approach the problem in a different way. When they know that they are in "one of those moods," they let their child know, also. They ask their child for a few minutes of "break-time" before discussing something or making some decision. This is a difficult approach to handle, since many times our mood won't even allow us to request the break-time. But when we can do it, and it is successful, we develop an excellent modeling situation for our child. We show him a way of temporarily dealing with his own moods. Hopefully, he will recognize that there are times when he should "take a deep breath" before discussing something or making some decision.

Each time we react to our child's behavior, we are communicating information. Our actions tell him whether we approve or disapprove of what he has done. To a large degree, our child uses our reactions as an indication of what he should do in the future. The more consistent we are, the easier it will be for him to learn what we desire. This rapid learning will have very beneficial effects for our child. The more often he behaves as we desire, the more likely we are to be loving, affectionate, and warm—which, in turn, means that we will be people *he* will enjoy being with.

Consistency—plain, not so simple, but very important.

Making—and
Living
with—Their
Own Decision

One of the most sought after behaviors parents wish to instill within their children is that of independent thinking. They want their children to be self-directed—to be able to monitor their own behavior. They want them to make appropriate decisions about their own behavior—to rely on their own judgment—particularly when their parents are not around to help them judge. They want their children to analyze problem situations and come up with conclusions and decisions they will feel comfortable living with.

Eventually, each child will be called on to make decisions about his own behavior, and what he comes up with may result in a paramount change in his life. It is the responsibility of the child's parents to teach him ways of making these decisions, not necessarily what decisions to make or which road he should take, but how to judge for himself what are the potential consequences—good or bad—of his choices.

There is a double purpose for this section. First, I want to present an idea that, admittedly, only scratches the surface of the complex behavior of decision making. As brief as my statement will be, I believe it is a start in the right direction. Second, I want to present a case to you. It depicts a decision a lovely young girl made about her own future. It is an unhappy case, but I think you will agree that the child was quite unhappy. One can only guess whether she thought carefully about the decision she eventually made. With the increasing number of young people who are making the same decision, the case may be representative of the times. If so, we should be aware of its possibility. Dr. Wesley Becker states:[21]

> "Our long(er) range goal is to teach a child to guide his own behavior, make good decisions, reason clearly about his choices and consequences, solve problems on his own, and plan ahead."

Just about everything I have talked about so far has been directed toward helping you teach your child to eventually govern his own behavior. By your actions and reactions you are teaching your child that his behavior has consequences or outcomes. He learns that his crying results in your comfort and assistance. He learns that experimenting with matches or electric sockets results in your disapproval. He learns that he can avoid your disapproval by avoiding the matches and sockets. In essence, these experiences teach him that things happen as a result of what *he does*. Eventually, he learns to *predict* the outcomes of what he does.

Once again, Dr. Becker states:[21]

> *"When a child is taught the rules about consequences of his own behavior*, he can make better decisions for himself when his parents are not there."

Before a child can learn to predict the outcomes of his behavior, he must first learn that his behavior has purpose—that things do happen as a result of what he does. He must learn that there are reasonably consistent consequences to his actions. Once learned, the child begins to realize that he has choices and that he can, to a degree, control the consequences of his behavior. As I see it, this realization is the necessary first step in the complex behavior of decision making. Again, this is what we have been talking about from the beginning of the book. Our reactions teach the child that not only are there reactions, but that he has something to say about the reactions.

Consider for a moment what you think about when you are faced with making a decision about your own behavior. Isn't it true that most of the time you carefully weigh the pros and cons of your potential action? By and large, the decision you make is based on the results of

---

[21] Becker, op cit., p. 144.

your analysis. I believe, ideally, this is what we want our children to do. From the very simple, "Should I or should I not play with Mom's perfume?" to the more complex and serious, "Should I or should I not experiment with that drug?", we want our children to be able to consider what will happen as a result of their doing or not doing. As Dr. Becker suggests, once a child learns that there are consequences to his behavior, he will be able to make better decisions for himself.

What you and I do, as parents, is to teach our child that there is a relationship between his actions and the environment's reactions. The more clear and consistent our communication is with our child, the easier it will be for him to learn this relationship. We owe it to our child to be as clear and consistent and communicative as is humanly possible. This helps him to be able to predict. This helps him learn how to make his own decisions.

He must live with his own decisions. We must help him understand what his decisions will likely mean to himself and his own life.

Suzie

At school, Suzie was a well-behaved, cooperative, 13-year-old young lady. She was very popular and was always considered a leader in her class. Her school work was better than average. With the exception of an occasional tardy entrance to class, her behavior was considered commendable. Apparently, however, she behaved quite differently at home.

I received a call from her mother asking for some help because of some difficulty she was having with Suzie. According to Mother, there was considerable fighting between Suzie and her parents. Although this had been going on for about a year, it was presently out of hand. The mother was also worried because Suzie was staying away from home for longer periods of time than ever before. She would not come home from school until 5:00 or 5:30, and she would leave the house almost immediately after dinner. She would indicate that she was going to do her homework over at a friend's house or else she would say "something had come up."

Mother did not like Suzie's friends and continually asked her to keep them away from the house. Recently, there had been some delinquency problems in the neighborhood and Suzie's mother, being concerned, wanted her to be in the house as much as possible. This point caused endless friction between Mother and daughter.

Conversation between Suzie and her father had completely broken down. Unless he threatened some form of punishment, they did not speak to one another. The communication between Suzie and her mother was strained and usually resulted in an argument. Any request made of the daughter required "at least five repetitions," and unless the request was made in a harsh tone, she would not carry it out. There apparently was a complete absence of any affection demonstrated by Suzie, although her father made continual demands for some sign of love. She had to be reminded to say good night, and she usually left for school without a word to either parent. When she was home, the door to her room was often locked, and she spent most of her time talking on the telephone. She rarely brought friends to the house for "fear her parents would embarrass her." However, when some of her friends did join her at home, the mother and daughter usually got into an argument over noise and offensive language. This language was particularly annoying to Suzie's parents, for they were often called "weird, gross, and queer." Suzie had also become "involved" with a boy from school, and they were spending a good deal of time together. She was expressly forbidden to have the young man at the house when her parents were away. The mother, however, felt certain he had been over several evenings when she and her husband were out.

It was quite evident that Suzie was not very fond of her parents. She did not seem to respond favorably to what little affection was being given. She no longer appeared to care or to listen to what her parents wanted. It was equally apparent that Suzie was receiving considerable attention from her friends. Presently, her parents were unable to compete with them. What little control the parents had over Suzie's behavior was through punishment, and even this was fast becoming ineffective. They were upset and confused.

"How do you know what to do?" the father questioned as he paced back and forth in the living room. "Everyone talks about using common sense—about how easy it is to bring up kids. If one more of my friends tells me all I have to do is this and that and everything will work out fine, I think I'll punch him. And I'll tell you something else," he paused for a moment, then looked directly at me, "you psychologists haven't helped us. You pick up one book and you are told to do one thing. Then a second book tells you something else, and a third says something different than the other two. We did what we thought was right," he continued. "I mean, what the hell . . . we didn't set out to end up in this situation!"

His tone was highly elevated, and his gestures reflected his anger. I sat quietly and listened to what he wanted to say. There were a few moments when I was not certain what he was going to do. After about 15 minutes, he abruptly stopped talking and sat down next to his wife. He took a deep breath and placed one of his hands over his eyes. His wife looked toward me and then at her husband. She gently slipped her right arm around his back. For many "long" minutes, the only audible sound was the drumming noise coming from the refrigerator.

The parents had gotten themselves into a difficult situation. I thought to myself—if only they hadn't waited so long to look at their daughter's behavior and the way they responded to it. Perhaps, had they spent some time making things more pleasant for themselves and Suzie, they could now compete and share with those who were the moving forces in her life. But the reality of the situation dictated otherwise. Through their admitted use of extensive punishment, the parents had become disliked, and Suzie was learning to avoid them. In place of looking at their own behavior, they just waited for her to change. Instead of discussing differences, they maintained their own position and waited for her to "come around."

But because of the pressure that had built up in recent weeks, they could no longer wait. "If we can't find a way to bring us together," Mother said, "I hate to think what things will be like in a few years."

Suzie's behavior had become so disruptive, so unpleasant, that the parents were forced to take a serious look at their situation. As a result of what they saw, they were united in their determination to bring about a change. There was an almost total absence of any disagreement between them. They were at the point where they were willing to take any advice or suggestions offered. The problem was determining the nature of the advice. Maybe Suzie could help.

Suzie was strikingly pretty. She had the dress and mannerisms of the times. Her language was often uninterpretable—she used expressions that I had never heard before. But we talked. She translated for me and appeared to enjoy the opportunity to do so. She was glib and friendly, but intently serious about her present situation. She did not like what was going on at home. She made that point several times. Inference was unnecessary; the complaints, accusations, and dissatisfactions were clearly and precisely stated. There was the sound of ultimatums, of "if-then" statements that would have been disturbing to her parents.

"Have you talked to your parents about the way you feel?" I asked. "Why," she answered, "I know what they would say!" When we concluded our conversation, she asked if we were going to meet again. "Yes, if you would like," I responded. She said, "Please."

"Do you think she is ready to change?" Mother asked.

"Not unless someone starts talking to someone," was my qualified answer.

Mother, Father, and I sat in the living room and began to talk. We talked about how important it is for a home to be a pleasant place. We talked about the effects that yelling and punishing have on making a home a pleasant place. We talked about friends and peers and the reinforcement they offer, and the effects they can have when parents fail to reinforce. We talked about love and respect and consideration, and how these are taught to children by parents who also love, respect, and consider. We talked about reinforcing children for their good behavior with attention and affection and the possibility of observing that behavior when there is no reinforcement. We talked about how difficult it can be to teach our children desired behaviors, but also what can happen when we allow others to do most of the teaching for us. We talked about how important it is for parents to look at what they are doing and to see what their children are learning as a result of their actions.

Our conversation was guarded. The parents were having a difficult time looking at their own behavior. But their effort was there, and one could sense a hint of progress. I mentioned to them that I had asked Suzie to compile a list describing the behaviors of her parents, and to specify those that she liked and disliked. We had to get conversation started, and I suggested that the parents do the same regarding their daughter's behavior. They readily agreed.

Suzie was sitting at the breakfast table when I arrived. As she looked up toward me, I could see that something about her had changed from our first meeting. Although noticeable, this difference was elusive—her dress, facial expression, the way she sat, something—but I couldn't determine what it was. As she handed me her lists, I asked her if there was anything she wanted to talk to me about or if she might want to ask any questions. With a half-smile, she quietly said, "No." I suspected that the difference was "within" me, and that explanation was partially satisfying. I began reading the lists while she watched me.

I dislike:

When my Mom gets nervous all the time and blames it on other people.

When she screams and yells at me—especially when I don't understand why.

When my Mom babies me and doesn't let me do things without a good reason or without any reason at all.

When my Dad always has to know who I am talking to on the phone and things that aren't even his business.

When my Dad thinks he's tough and hits me without talking things out.

When my Dad makes me kiss him all the time.

When my Mom screams her head off for dumb reasons in front of my friends.

When they make me do things for them all the time just 'cause they're too lazy to do it themselves.

When they purposely blame things on me when they know it's not the truth and I tell them that they know it's not the truth, but they are just saying it to make me mad, and when I do get mad, they yell at me.

When my Mom says "no" just because she feels like it.

When my Mom has to know everything.

When she tells me I can't wear something even when I know it would be all right to wear it and I want to.

When my Dad bugs me about my table manners when his aren't the greatest either.

When my Dad goes on my Mom's side just because he wants to.

When they both remind me to do something 10 times.

When my Mom has to know where I am going all the time.

I would like for my Dad to leave me alone when he knows I'm being bugged by him.

I would like for them to stop postponing things to the last minute or until it is too late.

I would like my parents to listen to me instead of laughing in my face.

There are more, but these are most important.

She did not say a word while I read the list. When I looked up from the material, she was staring directly at me. "You think my parents are going to be different just because you're here?" she asked rhetorically.

I told her that her parents and I had had some good discussions, and I sincerely believed that there would be a strong positive change. They had expressed a desire to do something to make everyone happier. Suzie continued to look at me, but did not respond. "Sometimes," I added, "parents believe they are doing what is right for their child, when their actions sometimes convey just the opposite message. That can cause some confusion and misunderstanding. When there is some dissatisfaction because of another person's actions, there is usually some discussion about the dissatisfactions. In that way, no one has to guess what is bothering the other person. But you and your parents have had difficulty talking with one another, and this is one area where I hope to help."

Any response from her would have been welcomed. Instead, she remained silent, staring at the lists. She kept running her fingers across her bottom lip while she appeared to read what she had written. Finally, she sat back in her chair, looked up at me, and smiled. I waited, but again she said nothing. I returned her smile and suggested that we meet again tomorrow. She said, "Okay," as she walked me to the front door.

On the way back to my office, I thought about Suzie's silence. I called Mother and asked if anything unusual had happened in the past 24 hours. She told me everything had gone pretty well. The entire family had spent a quiet evening at home with Suzie in her room all of the time. As I hung up, I couldn't help reflecting on the disconcerting feeling that I was experiencing. I lost it, however, in the shuffle of other problems.

There are times when the telephone is an unwelcomed necessity. This is true when it rings at a time when social conversation is unlikely. Had it been another evening, perhaps Suzie's name would not have come instantly to mind, and I would not have experienced a very sharp, uncomfortable sensation from my stomach. But her name and the physical feedback were there—and so was her mother's voice.

"We have a problem," she whispered as if to conceal her words from a third party, "I'm sorry to bother you at this hour, but my husband and I aren't certain what to do." I assured her that she should have called and urged her to continue.

"I promised Suzie that I would take her and some friends to a movie tonight. We had a small argument about what time to be home; I'm not certain that it was ever resolved. Anyway, we left the house to go for her friends." The mother's conversation was almost inaudible. I heard a click, as if someone had picked up an extension phone. It turned out to be her husband, who had joined the conversation. His hello was as quiet and somber as his wife's. The mother continued, "We did not talk to each other until all the other children had been picked up. As we neared the theater, I calmly reminded Suzie to be home no later than ten o'clock. I was trying to be very nice about telling her. But as soon as I had finished, she looked toward me and angrily said that she would come home when she felt like it. I tried to ignore her tone and simply said that her father and I had some plans, and we wanted her home by 10 p.m."

"She began to scream at me. She used such vile language that I was speechless. I have never heard her say anything like it before. Even her friends were surprised by the outburst. I was so angry, so shocked, that I began shaking. I screamed at her never to talk that way again to me or anyone. She was expressionless, and she said nothing. I am afraid that I really yelled at her. I began to feel badly at the fact that I had completely lost my temper."

"We arrived at the theater, and everyone left the car. I wanted to remind Suzie once more, but thought better of it. I wanted to say something about our argument but, before I had a chance, she turned and pointed her finger at me. She called me a queer and a bitch and then ran toward her friends—laughing. I couldn't contain myself any longer. I jumped from the car and ran to the line where she was standing. I grabbed her arm and pulled her into the car. She began to cry, and that was unusual. I can't remember the last time I saw her cry. When we arrived home, she darted from the car—still crying. She ran past her father and went upstairs, violently shutting the door to her room. My husband looked at me with astonishment. I just shook my head as if to say, "Don't ask." Suddenly we heard a horrible crash followed by screaming and the yelling of incoherent statements. My husband ran up the stairs and opened Suzie's door. She was standing at the foot of the bed holding a large piece of glass in her hand from the broken mirror that was all over the floor."

"I didn't recognize my own daughter," Suzie's father began. "She just stood there looking at me—holding the glass. Her eyes were wide open. She was trembling. Her bottom lip stuck out. She was as white as a sheet. I was scared. I was really scared. I've never seen her like that—I've never seen anyone like that. I took a step toward her. My hand was held out asking for the glass. She dropped it, turned her back toward me, and collapsed on the bed. She was crying heavily as I walked to her. I was terribly confused as to what to do. I turned the ceiling light off and the small bed lamp on. Then I waited for a few minutes to see if she was going to say anything to me, but she didn't. I softly told her that I would be downstairs if she needed me. Her sobbing had almost stopped, but her body was moving spasmodically. I stayed for a few more minutes until she was resting comfortably."

"How is she now?" I asked.

"She is quiet. In fact, she is cleaning up her room," Father answered. "She seems all right."

There was silence, and they seemed to be waiting for me to respond. But I, too, was waiting—waiting for my training and experience to tell me what to say. Our silence and my delay was interrupted by the father's quiet, saddened voice, "I just checked. She is fast asleep." "Well, we won't bother her now," I said. "I will meet with her tomorrow as planned and see if she will tell me something about what happened. Afterward, you and I can get together and talk."

The parents agreed, and as we began to say good-bye, the father said, "I can't believe that we taught her to do this, I just can't accept it. We may have taught her to do some things, but certainly not this—no, not this."

"No one is ever going to suggest that you and your wife taught Suzie to behave the way she did this evening," I immediately responded. "Her behavior was a result of many people and many different circumstances that have been going on for years. Your child's behavior has been continually responded to and shaped for 13 years. There have been many influences, other than yours, that have played a part in what occurred."

"The problem, as I see it, is that many parents do not take a look at their child's behavior until something 'bad' happens. Then they become concerned. They do not watch their own behavior or check to see the influences it may be having on their child's behavior. They take the easy way out. There is no preplanning—no preventive medicine."

"We do not go out of our way to recognize 'good' behavior. We do not view our children's behavior in the light of their total environment. We want them to do certain things, to wear certain things, to be certain ways, without considering the influences that others may be having on those same behaviors. We let time slip through our fingers. We wait too long. We do not ask our children for the feedback that would help us to determine the type of job we are doing. We do not communicate. Then one day they 'come home' with undesired behaviors. They no longer respond to us. They begin to question our methods of responding to them, for they observe others using different methods. Explanations such as, 'because I told you so,' or 'because I'm your father,' are no longer accepted. Our threats and punishments are less effective, even challenged, for they must compete against the more positive attention from others. The yelling, screaming, demanding regimentation of the home comes up against the absence of yelling, screaming, and regimentation away from home."

"For many of us, these problems never occur. The environment is good to us. It teaches our children just about what we had intended. We can get by without the preplanning, without the preventive medicine— but that is a big gamble to take. Relying on others to teach our children desired behavior is risky. But this is what we do when we fail to teach what we want. This is what we do when we fail to provide affection and appreciation for 'good' behaviors but, instead, ignore them, while attending to those that bother us. This is what happens when we fail to make the home a pleasant place to be."

In Suzie's case, the gamble was lost. The phone conversation early the following morning was brief and to the point. It only takes a few words to convey unpleasant information. Sometime during the night, Suzie had left home. She had taken some clothes, a few sandwiches, and what was estimated to be about $20. The police had been contacted, as had some of her friends. One of her girl friends remembered hearing something about going to Los Angeles, but she assumed Suzie was "only kidding."

About three weeks later, the mother called and told me that they had received an unsigned postcard mailed from Los Angeles. It said, "I'm fine. Am staying with friends." There was no return address or any information that would help locate Suzie. Nevertheless, her father had flown to Los Angeles. He wanted to show the card to the police to see if they could help. He had been there for several days, but had met with little success. The police were not very optimistic and suggested that he return home.

"We will do the best we can," they told him, "but it won't be easy. We have a large number of 'Suzies' in Los Angeles."

Getting Away and Getting It Together

Just think, tomorrow you and your spouse are leaving for a two-week vacation. Just the two of you, for two glorious weeks—Paris, Rome, and Honolulu. You've hired a good baby-sitter for the kids, and you know they will be just fine. Two weeks of fun, relaxation, and excitement. You will be able to sleep as late as you want. You will be able to go anywhere and do anything you desire. No strings attached. No holds barred. (A rich uncle has made all of this possible.)

You don't believe all of that? How about three days in Ithaca? Still no? Okay, how about a quiet evening for just the two of you at your favorite restaurant? One hour to watch a special TV show? How about a five-minute nap?

Sit back for a moment and think about all the things I have asked you to consider. You are going to try to catch your kids doing something good. When you do you are going to reinforce them. You are going to be very consistent in the ways you react to your children's behavior. You are not going to scream or yell. You are going to be calm and relaxed. You are going to ignore behavior that is annoying to you instead of reacting to it. You are going to plan which behaviors you want your child to do and which ones you would like him not to do. If you have to, you will use punishment but, again, you will be calm. After punishing, you are going to look for an alternative behavior that

112

can be reinforced so you won't have to use so much punishment. You are going to do a good job, so you will try to stay "on your toes" for the greater part of your waking day. But, you say, your child is not the only one in your family? Someone is coming home for dinner? You've got to fix yourself up. Perhaps, tonight is the night that someone's boss is coming over for dinner—and he's bringing his wife, whom you have never met. Find the dog, he has to be fed. Where is the dog? Not in the living room?! "It can't be five o'clock already—can it?" Yes, Virginia, it certainly can be.

You may not be able to muster two weeks in Paris or even three days in Ithaca. Well, how about one hour a day so that you can unwind—read, relax, do something different, anything, so long as you can get out from under. Oh, you've talked about that before. Have you done anything about it? Well, talk again, only this time do something about it. That one hour a day, at least one hour, is necessary—not only for you, but also for your children. Don't say it can't be done. Start figuring out a way to make it happen.

What are your chances for doing all that I have suggested if you are presently climbing the proverbial wall? Fat chance? How consistent can you be when that wall is about ready to tumble? How anxious are you going to be to catch little Billy doing something good when your disposition makes boiling an egg a major production?

Solution? Find yourself some free time. Devote at least one hour a day to *you*. Try to get out of the house for a little while. Go look at a new dress or sport coat or a new spatula. Even if you don't buy anything, at least go look. Instead of having a peanut butter and jelly sandwich for lunch at home, go to a drugstore for the same thing—assuming you can find one that still serves food. Have a one-person picnic in the backyard while the kids are napping. Go build a snowman or smell some flowers. Anything, only get yourself some free time. Don't say it can't be done. Find a way to make it happen. It may be the best free therapy you've ever had.

A free time period is critical. Without it you will have a very difficult time teaching what you desire. I haven't talked a great deal about attitudes and emotions, but this is a perfect place. Being pleasant and affectionate, in part, is a result of your present mood. And your mood is determined to a degree by what you face during the day. Many of us do wake up "on the wrong side of the bed" every once in a while. But for the most part, most of us are in pretty good shape after the first cup of coffee or glass of juice. Then we begin to face the daily routine. If the routine goes well we can handle most anything. But if events occur that begin to chip away at our pleasantness, we can go down hill fairly quickly. We start giving in to small, annoying behaviors. We let our frustrations get the best of us. Everything just seems to go backward. Break-time! Don't just take a deep breath and count to 10. Find yourself a sanctum—be it your basement, backyard, or bathroom.

One hour a day is not two weeks in Paris, but it can help. Don't say it can't be done. Do it!

Keeping Track of What Is Going On

Parents I work with are given homework assignments. Usually, I do not see them the second time until their assignments have been completed. They realize very quickly that before we can make changes for the better, I need not only their cooperation, but also some very important information. They also realize that the majority of the behaviors they are concerned with cannot be changed in my office. They know, after a few minutes of talking, that they are going to be the therapists, and their home will be the place where the teaching and changing will take place.

After briefly talking about some of the developmental aspects of their childern's behavior, we begin to discuss the present-day problems they are concerned about. Our discussions focus on three things. First, what is the child presently doing that you would prefer he no longer do? Second, what is the child not doing that you would like for him to do? Third, how do you react to his behavior? There are, of course, other things we talk about, but those three items are our basic points of early concentration.

Parents usually need some help with learning how to describe their children's behavior as well as their own reactions to the behavior. Most of us are not trained to be very precise and objective when describing certain events pertaining to our children, yet we are called on to be so on occasion. For example, our pediatrician asks us to keep track of our child's temperature when the child is not feeling well. Rarely do we report to the doctor that our child's fever is "very high." We are usually much more specific. When the doctor asks us to describe where our child is experiencing pain, we make an earnest effort to describe the exact location, the length of time the pain has been occurring, and perhaps what we have already done to relieve the pain—aspirin or bed. This type of specificity is often very helpful to the physician, and it is a must for the behavioral psychologist.

Generally, the first homework assignment involves the parents keeping a running account or diary of two things. First, what is the child doing that you no longer want him to do, and second, how do you react to these behaviors? The parents are requested to carry a piece of paper and pencil around with them, and they are asked to write down exactly what happened and how they reacted to the behavior. Here are some examples:

Time	Behavior	Reaction
7:45 a.m.	Johnny was told to get dressed. He said, "No."	I took him by the hand and dressed him.
8:00 a.m.	He asked for a bowl of cereal, but he refused to eat it when it was given. He said he wanted an egg.	I told him he had to eat what was given to him. Then I made him an egg. He did eat the egg.
2:00 p.m.	Mary and Billy began fighting over a toy. Mary had it first.	I told them that I would take the toy away unless they shared it. They said they would, so they were allowed to play with it.
7:30 p.m.	Billy was told it was bedtime. He refused to go, and he began to cry. I told him he would have to go to bed regardless of his crying. He still cried.	After he cried for a few moments, I told him he was not being a very good boy, but he could stay up for 10 more minutes.
	After the 10 minutes were up he started to cry again.	I put him to bed. He cried for a few minutes, then he fell asleep.

Notice that the descriptions offered in the above examples are quite clear. You and I should have little difficulty determining what happened. Let me present a few more examples that are not quite as clear. See if you can tell what actually happened.

Time	Behavior	Reaction
7:30 a.m.	Billy became very *obstinate*. He refused to *cooperate*.	I got very *upset* and I am afraid I *displayed* my *anger*.
9:00 a.m.	Mary was very *frustrated* over her father's indecision. She *pouted* the rest of the day.	I became *annoyed*, but I *comforted* her.
6:00 p.m.	Billy *showed* us he was *not ready* for any *responsibility*.	We *punished* him.

The italicized terms are certainly common ones and most of us use them frequently. There isn't anything wrong with the terms other than the possibility that you and I might not know what the parent means when he or she uses them. If the parent would tell us what Billy did when he became obstinate, or what he did that showed he wasn't ready for responsibility, we would have much more information. Similarly, it would be helpful to know what the parent did when she became angered, or when she comforted or punished her child. I'm certain Mother knows what she did when she comforted or punished, but would she be able to recall her specific reactions several days later? Would she be able to discuss accurately her reactions with another party?

If you are having some sort of problem, you will be getting off on the right foot if you carefully describe what the problem is and how you are responding to it. Your diary will help you know what is actually going on.

The next homework assignment deals exclusively with desired behavior and how it is reacted to. The parents do two things. First, they are to list some behaviors they would like their children *to do*—"I would like for him to clean up his room," or "I want him to share his toys with his sister." Watch yourself with this task, for you may end up writing something down that you *do not* want him to do—"I would like for him to *stop* grabbing toys," or "I want him to *stop* keeping his room in such a mess." Neither one of these last examples describe a behavior to increase. The second thing the parents do is to take their pencil and paper and begin writing down as many "small" good things their child does during the day. (Don't be too surprised if you begin to see many helpful and considerate behaviors that you have been accidentally ignoring.) After this has been done for several days, the parents begin to develop some behavior pairs. They particularly look for desired behaviors that are incompatible to some of the behaviors that are causing the parents concern. Once the behavior pairs are established, the parents' teaching program begins.

I urge you to take the needed time to develop this diary. It is true that at times, "One can't see the forest for the trees" and, in many cases, we have to step back for a while to see what is in front of us. Your diary will help you do just this. Spend a couple of hours at least for four or five days; watch yourself and your child at different times during these days; and if you are having some difficulty writing down what you think is important, ask your spouse or friend to help.

Those
Everyday
Troublesomes

One of the advantages afforded a child psychologist is his opportunities
for meeting and working with many parents. He can see that many
parents face the same types of problems. He can share with parents the
fact that the problems they are having have been experienced by many
others before them. Although this realization does not solve their own
difficulties, it does seem to ease some of their concern. Most
psychologists agree that there appears to be a kind of comforting
feeling experienced by an apprehensive parent once the parent realizes
that his child's behavior (or misbehavior) is not so unique. I remember
listening to two young mothers who were talking with one another at a
dinner party. One told her friend that she was very concerned about the
fact that her two-year-old daughter was constantly walking around the
house with a blanket in her hand, and she continued by saying she had
heard that this was a sign of insecurity. Her friend quickly responded
that both her youngsters had done the exact same thing, and they both
were happy, secure little larks. The friend also suggested that Mother
should "stop" reading so many *Peanuts* cartoons.

It is quite understandable why so many young parents become very
concerned about the "little" things their children do. We have all heard,
for many years, the warnings that certain behaviors are indicative of
very important psychological things. When parents see one of these

behaviors, they are often admonished—"Don't become overly alarmed, but something very serious may be going on *inside* your child." Hardly a month goes by when I do not see headlines in a sensational magazine or newspaper offering to its reader—"What you can learn about your son's personality by watching the way he blinks his eyes?" Or, "Does your infant daughter really love you or is she just interested in your milk? Take this quickie test and find out."

I believe the so-called everyday psychology that surrounds us has made many parents feel uptight about reacting and relating to their children. Depending on which article you read, it seems as if the parent is going to make some kind of mistake, regardless of what she does. With all the problems these articles tell us about, I am amazed at the number of children who make it!

Most assuredly, if you see that your child is persistently engaging in a behavior that you do not understand, and you have the slightest doubt about the behavior, check with your family physician. He can advise you about the behavior, and there is a good chance that he will either be able to help you with the problem or suggest the name of a psychologist or psychiatrist if such action is warranted.

But, at the same time, please keep in mind that many children walk around the house with blankets, thumbs, and bottles in their mouths, yet as the old saying goes, relatively few people manifest the same behaviors when they stand in front of the altar (although some people probably would like to). Lots of children have little rituals that they go through when coming home from school, or eating, or going to bed, and these patterns or habits are rarely anything more than just patterns, habits, or rituals. Simply because a child wants to have his vegetables on one side of the plate and the meat on the other, or he occasionally rocks in his crib, or says "No!" to his mother, or he uses a "four-letter word," or he takes a wooden hammer and breaks a doll that somehow resembles his father, or draws a picture of his mother—without any arms—and in purple, does not mean the child is ready for the couch. A friend became very concerned about the fact that her three-year-old all of a sudden began drinking her milk from a baby bottle. (Her friendly neighbor told her that this was a sign of "regression!!") Mother's concern eased only when she realized that her older daughter was modeling her newborn daughter's behavior. She relaxed, said thank you to her neighbor, paid no attention to the "new" behavior, and it stopped as quickly as it started. Another parent felt certain she had done something terribly wrong to her daughter while bathing her and that this was somehow responsible for the fact that the daughter refused to go swimming in the family pool. Apparently, the child overcame the conjectured "trauma" during the winter, for the child was swimming like a fish the following summer. I've talked with many parents who become highly concerned about their child's apparent lack of interest in painting, riding bicycles, playing baseball, or having stories read to them before bedtime as if it were "abnormal" not to have these interests. On the other hand, some parents are just as concerned about "too much" interest in bugs, certain types of clothes, or believe it or not, helping Mother with the dinner dishes.

Some parents are so concerned about doing something that will irreversibly harm their child's "psyche" that they have forgotten how to have fun being a parent. The simple truth is that most parents do a good job. Certainly, they do things on occasion that they think better of later, but this overconcern and uptightness is just not warranted. Relax! Granted your child may be doing something you would prefer that he not do. Okay, it does not mean that your child is going to grow up to be ODD! Relax, sit back in an easy chair, and look carefully at what he is doing. Now, look carefully at what you are doing. Don't fall into the "feel guilty syndrome": "Tell me what I have done wrong; I know I've done something wrong; I feel so terrible about doing whatever I did that I shouldn't have done." Once more, relax. Look at the behavior, consider how you have been reacting to it. If you get stuck, talk to a professional about what is going on. There is a good chance that the problem is not as serious as you are making yourself think.

STRICT, PERMISSIVE, OR A COMBINATION

There aren't any set rules, at least agreed on by everyone, as to how cooperative a child should be, or how well mannered a child should be at the dinner table, or as to what age a child should be toilet trained, or any number of other "should-be's." These questions or decisions as to what children should do, are individual ones, answerable only by the individual parent—and answerable only after the parent has considered his own child. Ultimately, the parent should require for his child only that which he sincerely believes is best for his child.

But how exacting or stringent should a parent be when teaching his determined "should-be's?" How definite or rigid should the parental attitude be when deciding what is best for his child? Is there room for flexibility?

Dr. Benjamin Spock states:[22]

> "I think that good parents who naturally lean toward strictness should stick to their guns and raise their children that way. Moderate strictness—in the sense of requiring good manners, prompt obedience, orderliness—is not harmful to children so long as the parents are basically kind and so long as the children are growing up happy and friendly. But strictness *is* harmful when the parents are overbearing, harsh, chronically disapproving, and make no allowances for a child's age and individuality. Parents who incline to an easygoing kind of management, who are satisfied with casual manners as long as the child's attitude is friendly, or who happen not to be particularly strict—for instance, about promptness or neatness—can also raise children who are considerate and cooperative, as long as parents are not afraid to be firm about those matters that do seem important to them."

Parents today are less apt to categorize themselves as being either strict or permissive. They recognize that neither term is completely suitable, for they are much more a combination of both. They are strict when they think it is appropriate, and they are permissive, in the sense of being flexible, when a situation calls for latitude. One of the critical aspects necessary for good, warm, family life is open and honest agreement among all members of the family. This agreement includes what behaviors are desirable. If joint agreement of the "should-be's" is difficult, then compromise is a must. If you will be considerate of your own behavior *and* considerate of your child's behavior, you will see that firmness and flexibility are workable partners.

TROUBLESOMES

I have selected a few behaviors that elicit a great number of questions from parents. We have looked at some of them already, but by briefly looking at them again, we will have a chance to review some important points.

[22] Benjamin Spock, *Baby and Child Care*, New York: Pocket Books, 1946, pp. 48-49.

Attention-Getting Crying

When parents can keep attention-getting crying to a minimum, they will be in a better position to determine if their child is experiencing real physical or emotional discomfort.

To keep attention-getting crying to a minimum you need to keep two things in mind. First, you must not react to the crying—you must see to it that the behavior does not result in any outcome for the child. The complete ignoring of attention-getting crying tells your child that the behavior is something you no longer want him to do. Second, you must teach your child a more desirable means of gaining your attention. Decide on an alternative behavior that is to replace the crying and attend to it frequently.

When you observe your child crying, check as carefully as possible his present physical state. If he has had a problem with a friend or relative and is upset, then see what you can do about it. Comfort your child, but avoid making a big issue out of it. If you see that his present physical and emotional state is not the problem, and the crying persists, then consider the possibility that he is crying because he has learned that you will react to him favorably when he does so. Remember, if your child has learned that one of the best and "easiest" ways of gaining your attention is by crying, then that is what he is going to do. By sticking with the above suggestions, you will not be eliminating crying. Instead, you will be helping your child learn a way of letting you know when he is experiencing real discomfort.

Dinner Table Behavior

All parents have various guidelines for dinner time behavior for their children. Some, for example, use Grandma's Rule where dessert or snacks are delayed or withheld until most of the main course has been eaten. Some parents send their children away from the dinner table if there is excessive fighting or fussing. And just about every parent has a reasonable time period set aside for dinner to be completed.

In many cases, dinner time problems arise because the parents have not clearly communicated their guidelines to their children—the children do not know what is expected of them; or, although the guidelines have been discussed, the parents do not consistently hold with what has been decided; or, without realizing it, the parents are accidentally maintaining the very behaviors that are responsible for their difficulties.

The first problem mentioned above is probably the easiest one to handle. If your child is old enough to understand your explanation, explain to him what you consider to be appropriate dinner time behavior. Try to be as explicit as possible. This assumes, of course, that you have determined some dinner time guidelines. If you haven't, you can't very well expect your child to know something that has yet to be determined. Remember also, your child will use you as a model. If you want him to eat slowly, and you eat quickly, he's probably not going to do what you want.

As to your consistency, suppose you use Grandma's Rule that dessert is withheld until the main course is eaten, but more times than not you do not keep to your rule. Again, it is unlikely that your child will do what you ask. Or, you make it known that fighting is not allowed at the table and that if it takes place, the party must leave the table. However, when it does occur, you fail to follow through with what has been agreed on. This approach is probably not going to eliminate fighting during dinner. I am not suggesting that you *always* withhold dessert or *always* send the child away from the table when the guidelines have not been adhered to. There may be some very appropriate extenuating circumstances, and you should take them into consideration. But when these circumstances are not evident, then you should consistently stick to what has been decided.

Finally, keep in mind that a child who is told 10 times to eat is being given a great deal of attention for *not* eating. As has been suggested, coaxing almost always works against you, for you end up attending to the very behavior you wish to decrease. Again, decide on and reinforce a behavior that is incompatible to the one that you would like to reduce. In this case, ignoring the noneating and attending to whatever eating you observe will make dinner time much more pleasant for you and will probably increase your child's eating at the same time.

Following Requests

One of the reasons why children often fail to follow their parents' requests is that many children have learned that little, if anything, happens as a result of their action *or* inaction.

A child is asked not to ride a bicycle that is too small for him. He still rides it despite his parent's request. After three or four more minutes, he is once again requested, perhaps told, not to ride the bike any more. He still rides it, voicing his opinion that he is not too heavy and he will not break the "dumb" thing. After two more times of being told and two more refusals to do what was told, the parent *stops* requesting and the child *continues* to ride.

A second child is asked to bring her father a book that is out of his reach. The child is engrossed in a favorite TV show. Nevertheless, she immediately brings the book to her father. He opens the book with no smile, no wink, no word of thanks, no nothing!

When teaching your child to follow requests, consider the following:

1. Do not request your child to do something unless you intend for him to do it. Consider the types of requests you are going to make and be certain that both you and your spouse agree that the request is considerate, appropriate and will be carried out.

2. When your child follows your request, no matter how simple or "small" the request might be, take a second to thank or praise his behavior. There is no way I can overemphasize the importance of the praise, attention, and "thanks" you give your child when he does what you have asked. It takes so little time on your part. A parent once asked me, "At what age is a child old enough to appreciate and understand a parent's thanks?" I told her I wasn't exactly certain, but that she should begin thanking her child for following requests the moment the child is brought home from the hospital. When you ask you four-*day*-old to go to sleep so you can get some rest, and he does, thank him!

3. A decision should be made as to what will happen if your child fails to follow one of your requests. The assumption is that you would not have made the request in the first place had you not wanted it carried out. This notion should be communicated to your child, for you will want him to learn that on the few occasions when you request something of him, he is to do what is asked.

4. Watch what your child is doing before a request is made of him. Try to avoid pulling your child away from something he is really enjoying when the forthcoming request is not a major one. When you are going to have to request that your child leave a very enjoyable activity for one that is less enjoyable, give him a few minutes warning signal that the request is going to be made. Give him a chance to get ready for the request.

Coming Home When Called

Many parents experience little difficulty when asking their children to come inside the house. Typical of these parents is their sense of consideration. They recognize that coming home sometimes means that their child must stop (at least temporarily) some activity that is most enjoyable. They let their child know that he will have to come home within five minutes instead of right away. When the child does arrive home, he is usually greeted warmly and, in many instances, the parents express an interest in the activities their child was enjoying. For many parents, the above approach is all that is necessary. Others, however, offer their child a few extra minutes of stay-up time when he comes in when first called. Some offer their child some additional TV time, or a special treat, or a quick game of checkers. There is almost always some reinforcement and it is usually just a warm "thanks."

When necessary, the parents also remove or withhold some reinforcement when the child fails to come in when called. He may have to go to bed a little earlier or lose a few minutes of TV time. Whenever the parent removes the reinforcement, there is conversation between the parent and the child. He is reminded of the consequences of his behavior, so that eventually he will be able to monitor his own actions. But above everything else, the parent is considerate, and it doesn't take much time for a child to realize and appreciate his parent's consideration *and* desires. This mutual appreciation and consideration serves to make the family relationship warm and close.

Toilet Training

If you talk to 10 parents you may think you have found 10 different ways to teach toilet training. Once you look carefully, however, at the 10 approaches, you will find some very common characteristics. Let me present an example from the Krumboltzes' book that depicts one mother's successful toilet training procedures.[23] There are some excellent suggestions in this short example.

When Danny was two years old his mother decided to begin toilet training him. Here is her report of how she proceeded.

I knew I had done a poor job in toilet training Danny's older sister

---

[23] Krumboltz, op. cit., p. 123.

when she was about two years old. I had gotten upset with her whenever she wet her pants. Then she would get upset when I got upset. It was an unhappy experience for both of us, and I was determined not to let this problem occur with Danny. The first step was getting Danny to have a success experience that I could reward. Whenever enough time had elapsed so that I could predict Danny was about to urinate, I would take him to the toilet. For two days we had no success. Finally on the third day after what seemed to be an interminable time he did urinate in the toilet. I immediately gave him a piece of candy and praised him liberally. From then on the task became rapidly easier. Every time Danny used the toilet successfully I gave him a piece of candy and expressed my genuine delight. When he wet his pants, he received no reward whatsoever. However, I was careful never to get upset or angry at his failures. Within a short period of time Danny seemed to have learned to use the toilet properly, announcing his readiness with the statement, "Toidy, Mommy." Accidents were infrequent and resulted mainly from poor timing. About this time I remember thinking to myself, "So far, so good. But what if he needs his mother around to reward him for each good performance all his life!" So once I thought he had the habit pretty well established, I gradually cut back on the candy even when he requested it. Instead I continued to praise him highly every time. Gradually over the next few weeks, I found I could reduce the number of times I praised him and I stopped giving him candy altogether. Danny was trained without either one of us getting emotionally upset. His rewards now come from knowing he can use the bathroom like a grownup and from the constant comfort of dry pants.

Although we can only guess how long it took Danny's mother to accomplish the training, not everyone will be so successful in what appears to be a very short period of time. Danny urinated in the toilet on the third day of Mother's program. Mom was pretty lucky! But regardless of the time in Danny's case, it is safe to say that his mother would have continued her approach of attempting to predict her son's behavior and then taking him to the toilet for as long as *her* patience allowed.

One of the necessary ingredients for successful toilet training is the *parents'* readiness—that is, unless the child trains himself, which does happen. Many authorities agree that parents often start toilet training their children too soon. Neither the child nor his parents are ready for the experience. If this happens, the experience will be unpleasant for everyone. If you become frustrated and upset, your child is going to be upset, and it is unlikely that an upset child is going to be very cooperative. If you become angry and express your anger, your punishment will become associated with toilet behavior, and your child will try the best he can to *avoid* the toilet. So before you begin, make certain you and your child are ready.

Notice that Danny's mother wanted, like all of us, to avoid an unhappy experience. To do this, she began to keep track of her son's wetting behavior in the hopes of predicting approximately when he would have to urinate. You can do this by either asking your child, or sometimes more successfully, occasionally feeling your child's training pants to see if they are wet. After several days of keeping a simple record of how many hours your child remains dry, you will have a pretty good idea of when you can expect him to wet again.

Mother then used her reinforcement when Danny used the toilet appropriately and withheld her reinforcement when he had an accident. Once Danny had many successes, Mother began to gradually reduce the use of her reinforcement.

One last point about toilet training before moving on. Behavioral psychologist have learned that the more often a behavior occurs and is immediately followed by reinforcement, the more rapid the behavior will be learned. One of the major difficulties with teaching correct toilet behavior is that a child does not urinate a great number of times during his waking hours. There may be periods of four or five hours between wettings. As such, the number of opportunities the parent has to use her reinforcement for the desired behavior is limited. Some parents have partially circumvented this problem by allowing their child to have almost unlimited access to water, milk, Kool Aid, or juice during the early states of toilet training. Before you try this, however, check with your family physician to see if he would advise against it for your child.

Bedtime—Getting Ready and Going

Some kids just seem to love to sleep. They do not have to be reminded or asked to go to bed—they are there before we know it. Others, however, want to prove that sleep is only for bears and the birds.

Every authority in the field of child psychology agrees that bedtime should not be associated with punishment, threatening, or scolding. For parents, this is sometimes easier said then done. Many of us do become upset when our child continually fails to go to bed when requested, and we react in ways that make us feel bad. Sometimes our frustration gets to a point where we find ourselves doing most anything that will enable *us* to *avoid* the discomfort experienced at bedtime hours. Our avoidance often takes the form of giving in; we fail to follow through with our predetermined guidelines for bedtime behavior. Ironically, the child learns that if he puts up enough of a fuss, his parents will not be able to tolerate the disruption. His disruption increases, and his parents' tolerance decreases. At that point, the cycle results in discomfort for everyone.

Now that I have painted a gloomy picture, let me quickly add that bedtime problems are not difficult to deal with. Most parents who are experiencing difficulty can bring about a change within a few days.

Bedtime problems occur as a result of how you react to your child when the bedtime hour comes. Although important, a precise, set bedtime hour, or playing your child's bedtime hour "by ear" is not the only issue to consider. What is of major importance is developing a bedtime atmosphere where you will have an easy time following through with your request that your child go to sleep.

Getting Him Ready. If you can avoid the "come hell or high water" 7:30 bedtime hour approach, you will be more likely to develop the atmosphere where your child's protesting will be minimal. This doesn't mean that you should not have a reasonably set bedtime hour, but it means that there will be times when you should be willing to adjust the hour to fit the activities of the moment. Your goal when getting your child ready for bed is to set the conditions so that he will be willing to go to bed when you say the time has come.

Most parents try to avoid placing their child in bed when he is right in the middle of a very enjoyable activity. They give their child a 15-minute or half-hour signal that bedtime is approaching. They allow their child to "ready himself" for bed. They use a very similar approach if their child has been very active immediately prior to the bedtime hour. They give their signal, and they spend time with the child to help him slow down. They've learned that placing an active child in bed—one who is not thrilled to be in bed in the first place—is not the approach to use. If you will play this part of getting him ready "by ear," chances are you will not begin to hear things from him that will make your goal difficult to attain.

If you know, from past experiences, that your child is going to ask you for several drinks of water, for many pieces of tissue, for milk and cookies, and then to go to the bathroom twice, take care of these desires before you put him in bed. If you haven't been doing this, and you suddenly begin to do so, you will probably find that your child will come up with some brand new request after he is in bed. If so, make a mental note of it and take care of it the following night *before* bed.

. . . and Going. Once your child's needs have been satisfied and he has had a chance to say good night to everyone, he should go off to bed. If all goes well he will be asleep within a very short period of time. But let us assume that he does not fall asleep right away, and you hear him crying or calling for you. Take a split second to think about his previous bedtime behaviors. If he *rarely* cries or calls for you when placed in bed, but suddenly begins to do so, *immediately* check to see if anything is wrong. Don't allow him to cry for 15 minutes and then go in to see him. There are two important reasons for this immediacy. First, of course, something may be wrong. It may be minor, but if he rarely cries, go see him right away. Perhaps it is cold in the room, or a light has been left on or off, or the wind is making unusual noises. Maybe he wants to say good night just once more, or remind you of the trip to the zoo tomorrow, or just look at your face before falling asleep. Second, there may be absolutely nothing wrong and for whatever reason he just starts crying. By allowing him to cry for 15 minutes and then going in to see him, you are reinforcing 15 minutes of crying. It is much more difficult to undo 15 minutes of "attention-getting" crying than 30 seconds of the same.

Now let us assume that your child *usually* cries a little—or a lot—when placed in bed. Assume also that in the past you have gone to him to see what was wrong and you found everything was okay. Quite possibly, you also found that his crying stopped when you came into the room or picked him up and that it started as soon as you left or put him down. If your split-second thought reminds you that this is probably happening again, there is a very good chance that you have been accidentally reinforcing his crying. To reduce the attention-getting bedtime crying, you must not respond to it. The child should be allowed to cry himself to sleep. Now I know that no one enjoys letting a child cry, particularly a young child. We always have the notion that he is trying to tell us something. In this case, he is probably telling you that he doesn't like the idea that you are not going to sit with him or carry him around. At some point in time, your child is going to have to learn to respect your determined bedtime hour. One of the best ways for him to learn this is to see that bedtime means bedtime, and you are more likely to convey this message by sticking to your guns. This means that once you place your child in bed, you should not walk back into the room to check on him—not while he is crying, at least. Again, please understand that there are exceptions to this firmness. If your child rarely cries or has been asleep for some time and he suddenly begins to cry, go to him immediately. If everything is fine, then leave immediately. If, by accident, you do reinforce a very brief period of attention-getting crying, you will be able to undo it without difficulty—and besides, your peace of mind is very important.

I believe that most psychologists agree with this approach. We differ on what age this approach should begin. Some suggest waiting until the child is six months old. Others suggest that the approach can be started much earlier, and I am in agreement with this latter group. Eventually, all parents teach their children that they will not come into their room each and every time crying is heard. You will not irreversibly harm your child's "psyche" or "personality" if you start a little before or a little after, say, six months of age. The longer you wait to teach him to respect your bedtime hour, the more attention-getting crying you will eventually have to deal with.

If you are having some difficulty with bedtime problems with an older child you might wish to try an approach that many parents have used very successfully. Extra stay-up time on weekends is a very strong reinforcer for many children, and it should be an easy reinforcer for you to use. The approach is very simple. Each night the child goes to bed when first asked—or when the hour of bedtime is present—the child earns 5, 10, or 15 minutes of extra stay-up time for nonschool nights. When he fails to go to bed when asked, he loses a similar amount of time for the weekends. This type of approach is especially effective when the child is asked to help set it up.

Finally, keep in mind that a little praise and recognition for appropriate bedtime behavior may be all that is needed to solve your problem. Even though there will be a long delay between bedtime behavior and reinforcement in the morning, your praise and appreciation can be very helpful. Some light conversation at the breakfast table about how much you sincerely appreciate your child's going to bed without any fuss can be just the solution.

A Closing Thought

You and I work very hard for experiences that result in pleasurable outcomes—activities that bring us pleasure that are worth experiencing again. These pleasures come dressed in many different packages. For one, the package is a trip to a foreign country, for another, a quiet dinner at home, for a third, a silent prayer before bed. But for many, the ultimate package is that planned, healthy, beautiful, six-pound bundle of life—that package Nature dutifully places in our hands. Pleasure, however, does not always accompany Nature's giving. Neither the child nor his parents are guaranteed anything. Instead, each must work for the other before pleasure is achieved. When this occurs, happiness in one of its fullest meanings is achieved. For happiness is a happy child—who, in turn, makes his parents happy—who, in turn keeps the cycle going. But the bias of this book states that the cycle must start with the parents, for the happy child must be made. It is doubtful that he is born that way. It is the parent who must initiate the cycle. It is the parent who must go out of his way to make things pleasurable, to teach what is desired, or else he gambles that others will teach what he, himself, intended.

Those, however, who start the cycle, who go out of their way, who work to recognize and praise desired behavior find the benefits worth the effort. For the happiness of a parent comes from the happiness he makes for his child—with that, the genesis of an unrivaled, lasting pleasure.

Glossary

Accidental Reinforcement. Providing reinforcement for a behavior when not meaning to increase it. For example, giving a child a lollipop while he is screaming for it. The screaming has been accidentally reinforced. It will probably occur again the next time something the child wants is withheld from him.

Appropriate Behavior. From the parents' standpoint, this is behavior that they would like to see occur more often. It is desired behavior. From the child's standpoint, it is any behavior that brings him positive reinforcement. For example, if a child discovers that crying instead of other behaviors brings him more attention, then crying is appropriate—it results in his parents' attention.

Attention. Recognizing the occurrence of a behavior and responding to it. There is verbal attention—"Thank you" (which is usually considered positive attention) or "Stop doing that!" (which is usually considered negative attention). Both positive and negative attention can result in the increase of a behavior, desirable or otherwise. There is also nonverbal attention—smiles, glances, gestures. Nonverbal attention can be as influential as verbal attention in increasing behavior, desirable or otherwise.

134

Behavior Pairs.   Two behaviors that cannot take place at the same time. They are incompatible to one another. A child cannot be sitting and standing at the same time. The behavior pair always consists of one desirable and one undesirable behavior; one behavior to be increased and one behavior to be decreased.

Consequences.   Events that take place immediately after behavior that can influence that behavior. Positive reinforcers and punishers are types of consequences.

(To) Decrease Behavior.   To get a behavior that is presently occurring to occur less often.

Determinants.   Events that are potentially responsible for the occurrence of a particular behavior.

Discriminate.   To tell the difference between two things that may be very much alike or quite different. Initially, a child calls everyone "Dada." After a while, he learns the difference between his father and mother—he learns to discriminate between the two and he calls one "Dada," and one "Mom" (and the one he calls Mom *is* his mother).

Environment.   Everything around us—people, places, things, events— that can influence what we do and feel.

Gradual Improvement.   Slowly getting better at doing something.

Ignoring Behavior.   Withholding all attention, recognition, positive reinforcement when a behavior takes place. *Note:* Withholding attention means withholding both verbal and nonverbal recognition. Glancing toward a child when he is doing something you wish to decrease *is not* ignoring the behavior. In fact, your occasional glance may be a form of occasional reinforcement which will increase the misbehavior. (See occasional reinforcement.)

Immediate Punishment.   Using punishment as soon as an undesired behavior takes place.

Immediate Reinforcement.   Using positive reinforcement as soon as a desired behavior takes place.

(To) Increase Behavior.   Getting a behavior that presently is occurring infrequently to occur more often.

Lawful Behavior. Behavior that occurs in an orderly and predictable fashion. The behavior follows consistent patterns. It is reliable and, given the necessary conditions, the behavior will occur in the same way time and time again.

Maintaining Behavior. Keeping behavior going once it has started to occur.

Modeling. Setting an example for someone. Often results in the imitation of the example.

Observable Behavior. Things that we do that can be seen or heard. Activities that can be counted and recorded.

Occasional Reinforcement. Reinforcement that is unpredictable, sometimes it comes and sometimes it doesn't come. Occasional reinforcement usually results in strong increases in behavior because we aren't certain when it is coming so our efforts persist.

Positive Reinforcement. A procedure used to increase the occurrence of a behavior. The procedure involves the application of a positive reinforcer immediately after the occurrence of a behavior.

Postive Reinforcer. Any thing, event, reaction, or activity you are willing to put our effort to obtain. Something we work hard to get. Any thing that is given immediately after a behavior that results in an increase of that behavior.

Praise. Positive recognition and attention. An act of expressing appreciation and thanks.

Predictable (Behavior). Being able to tell that something is going to happen before it actually does. Behavior that we are reasonably certain will take place in the future—often, the very near future.

Principle. A general rule that is backed by some scientific evidence.

Punishment. A procedure used to decrease the occurrence of behavior. It is generally agreed that there are two types of punishment. (1) The application of an aversive or unpleasant event immediately after the occurrence of a behavior—spanking. (2) The withholding or removing of a material positive reinforcer immediately after the occurrence of a behavior—withholding television privileges for a period of time.

Punisher. Any thing, event, reaction or activity you are willing to put out effort to avoid. Something we work hard to avoid. Any thing that is given immediately after a behavior that results in a decrease of that behavior.

Self-directed Behavior. Behavior that is presently being guided by the individual. The individual makes choices about his own behavior, once having learned what will likely happen as a result of his choice.

Shaping. Reinforcing gradual improvement of performance that eventually leads to the learning of a complex task.

Time-Out From Reinforcement. A procedure used to decrease the occurrence of a behavior. All reinforcement—material and social—is withheld for a brief period of time or until an appropriate behavior occurs.

Warning Signal. A verbal or nonverbal sign that a behavior is to stop. Precedes the use of punishment. Has been associated with punishment in the past and is presently used to indicate that if the behavior does not stop, punishment will be forthcoming.

Suggested Reading

For Parents:
(Most any bookstore will be happy to order these for you.)

Wesley Becker, *Parents are Teachers*. Research Press Company, Champaign, Ill.

Alvin Deibert and Alice Harmon, *New Tools for Changing Behavior*. Research Press Company, Champaign, Ill.

John and Helen Krumboltz, *Changing Children's Behavior*. Prentice Hall, Englewood Cliffs, N.J.

Clifford and Charles Madsen, *Parents/Children/Discipline: A Positive Approach*. Allyn & Bacon, Boston.

Gerald Patterson and Elizabeth Gullion, *Living With Children: New Methods for Parents and Teachers*. Research Press Company, Champaign, Ill.

For Teachers:
(College bookstores should have these.)

Wesley Becker, Siegfried Engelmann, and Don Thomas, *Teaching: A Course in Applied Psychology*. Science Research Associates, Chicago, Ill.

Don Bushell, Jr., *Classroom Behavior: A Little Book for Teachers*. Prentice-Hall, Englewood Cliffs, N.J.

R. Vance Hall, *Managing Behavior, Parts I, II, and III*. H & H Enterprises, Lawrence, Kansas.

Lloyd Homme, Attila Casanyi, Mary Ann Gonzales, and James Rechs, *How to Use Contingency Contracting in the Classroom*. Research Press Company, Champaign, Ill.

Beth Sulzer and G. Roy Mayer, *Behavior Modification for School Personnel*. The Dryden Press, Hinsdale, Ill.

Index